Reclaiming the Secret of Love

Reclaiming the Secret of Love

Feminism, Imagination and Sexual Difference

Ann Louise Gilligan

Edited by Katherine Zappone

Peter Lang
Oxford · Bern · Berlin · Bruxelles · New York · Wien

Bibliographic information published by Die Deutsche Nationalbibliothek
Die Deutsche Nationalbibliothek lists this publication in the Deutsche Nationalbibliografie; detailed bibliographic data is available on the Internet at http://dnb.d-nb.de.

A catalogue record for this book is available from the British Library.

Library of Congress Cataloging-in-Publication Data
Names: Gilligan, Ann Louise, author.
Title: Reclaiming the secret of love : feminism, imagination and sexual difference / Ann Louise Gilligan.
Description: Oxford ; New York : Peter Lang, [2021] | Includes bibliographical references and index.
Identifiers: LCCN 2020057964 (print) | LCCN 2020057965 (ebook) | ISBN 9781800792371 (paperback) | ISBN 9781800792388 (ebook) | ISBN 9781800792395 (epub) | ISBN 9781800792401 (mobi)
Subjects: LCSH: Feminism. | Imagination. | Sex role. | Women--Identity.
Classification: LCC HQ1155 .G525 2021 (print) | LCC HQ1155 (ebook) | DDC 305.42--dc23
LC record available at https://lccn.loc.gov/2020057964
LC ebook record available at https://lccn.loc.gov/2020057965

Cover design by Brian Melville for Peter Lang
Cover image: Gráinne Dowling (www.grainnedowling.ie)

ISBN 978-1-80079-237-1 (print) • ISBN 978-1-80079-238-8 (ePDF)
ISBN 978-1-80079-239-5 (ePub) • ISBN 978-1-80079-240-1 (mobi)

Published by Peter Lang Ltd, International Academic Publishers,
52 St Giles, Oxford, OX1 3LU, United Kingdom
oxford@peterlang.com, www.peterlang.com

This publication has been peer reviewed.

Contents

Permissions for Poetry and Art Images

Extract from A Grafted Tongue by John Montague from *New Collected Poems* (2012) reproduced by kind permission of the author's Estate and The Gallery Press. www.gallerypress.com.

Permission to quote from *Misogynist* by Michael Harding from *The Crack in the Emerald: New Irish Plays* (London: Nick Hern Books, 1990) by kind permission of the publisher. www.nickhernbooks.co.uk.

Permission to quote from We Are Damned, My Sisters by Nuala Ní Dhomhnaill, from *Selected Poems. Translated by Michael Hartnett* (Dublin: Raven Arts Press, 1988) by kind permission of the publisher.

Excerpt from "Letter to the Front" © Muriel Rukeyser from *The Collected Poems of Muriel Rukeyser*, 2005, University of Pittsburgh Press, by kind permission of William L. Rukeyser, in personal correspondence with Katherine Zappone.

Permission to quote from The Art of Grief by Eavan Boland from *A Time of Violence,* (Manchester UK: Carcanet Press, 1994) by kind permission of the publisher and by Norton Publishing.

Permission to quote from Home by Paula Meehan, from *As If By Magic: Selected Poems* (Dublin: Dedalus Press, 2020), by kind permission of the publisher.

Permission to quote Plays 1 by Brian Friel (London: Faber and Faber, 1996) by kind permission of the publisher.

Permission to quote from The Settle Bed by Seamus Heaney, from *Seeing Things* (London: Faber and Faber, 1991) by kind permission of the publisher and the family of Seamus Heaney.

Permission to quote from The Canton of Expectations by Seamus Heaney, from *New Selected Poems 1966–1987* (London: Faber and Faber, 1990) by kind permission of the publisher and the family of Seamus Heaney.

Permission to reproduce images from Sounding the Depths, a collaborative installation by Pauline Cummins and Louise Walsh. Images by kind permission of the artists, and the Irish Museum of Modern Art.

Acknowledgements

I know there are many people that Ann Louise would want me to thank, on her behalf. She never let a kindness pass, without expressing gratitude – one of her many attributes.

I shall begin by thanking Dr. Paul Downes, her friend and colleague of St. Patrick's College Drumcondra, Dublin City University, and a man she did not know when she wrote this. Paul was the one to 'discover' the value of her manuscript for the twenty-first century, when he expressed an interest to read it after her passing. He believed in its potential, and led me to Anthony Mason of Peter Lang. Ann Louise would have loved you, Tony. Dr. Anne Frances O'Reilly, another Pat's colleague and close friend and confidante of Ann Louise, assisted in getting permissions from the poets and playwrights that Ann Louise quotes. Anne Frances, a poet herself, spent hours and days on this project, because she knew how much it would mean to Ann Louise – her friend who was so fluent in the appreciation and teaching of poetry. I want to thank too Sarah Murphy, who worked closely with me to copy edit the manuscript, to ensure its technical beauty.

Two more folks from the Dublin City University family I know she would want me to thank. Dr. Daire Keogh, current President, colleague and friend who had the 'office next door' when they worked together. She would be so proud of you Daire. And Dr Brian MacCraith, past President of DCU, friend to me in my membership of the Irish government, and the man who honoured Ann Louise's professional legacy in so many ways.

Two colleagues of Boston College deserve special mention. Professor Thomas Groome, Ann Louise's doctoral advisor and friend, was so supportive of her writing of this manuscript. Professor Richard Kearney, her colleague and friend, inspired so much of Ann Louise's love for and understanding of the philosophy of the imagination, especially as found within the works of Paul Ricoeur.

I want to thank the artists – poetic, artistic and literary – who resourced Ann Louise's writing, and life. Very special thanks to: Gráinne

Dowling, Pauline Cummins, Louise Walsh, Nuala Ní Dhomhnaill, Eavan Bolan, Paula Meehan, Muriel Rukeyser, Seamus Heaney, Michael Harding and John Montague. I also want to express my gratitude to all of Ann Louise's students in Pat's and in The Shanty/An Cosán. You gave her life such vivacity and meaning.

Finally, family was very important to Ann Louise. I know that she would have acknowledged her sister June, and husband Michael, her brother Arthur and his wife Margaret, her nieces and nephews Sally, Hilda, Shane, Colin, Cait, and their spouses Bruce, Dermot, Muireann and Trina, and all their children.

Katherine Zappone

KATHERINE E. ZAPPONE

Foreword

Ann Louise Gilligan was always a woman ahead of her time. Her eyes, mind and heart were forever imaging the possible. Even after she was blinded by her first major brain haemorrhage in 2013, she practised the art of the *female imaginaire*[1] coupled with learning from key insights of neuroscience, to heal herself and begin to offer methodologies for others to do the same.[2]

She is my late spouse, lover, counsellor and best friend. When she wrote this manuscript in the late 1990s,[3] I typed and edited every word. It was not a heavy task. In fact, it was a joy to witness the ways in which she wove together dense philosophical ideas with her own praxis of love to invite creation of the new – in the classroom, community and public stage. Ann Louise's gift for communication, rooted in a profound understanding of the philosophy of the imagination, and a tenacious grasp of feminist theory of the late twentieth century, enabled her always to speak and to write a common language so that no one was left behind.

As Ann Louise outlines in the introduction, this book represents her life's work as an educational philosopher up to the point of its writing, starting in the aesthetic Parisian 1970s where she did a master's degree, through the liberatory and feminist 1980s of her PhD studies at Boston College, and her subsequent interrogations of how feminist theory, rooted

1 A concept developed by Luce Irigaray in her philosophical and psychological writings that had a profound influence on Ann Louise's own philosophy, teaching and social activism.

2 I am writing a book that incorporates this part of her philosophic journey, *Somewhere Between Grief and Joy* (to be published in 2022).

3 There was no date on the manuscript when we unearthed it after her passing in 2017. In light of the terrain it covers – footnotes and bibliography – mixed together with my own memory, this is my best guess.

in a practice of love, could motivate the becoming of female subjectivity as a prime source for individual, social and global change.

Ann Louise taught for over thirty years at St Patrick's College Drumcondra, Dublin City. It was known as one of the prime 'teacher training colleges' in Ireland, administered by the Vincentian Fathers, and managed by the Archbishop of Dublin. She was a 'teacher of teachers', an educator extraordinaire.

Her passion for the art of teaching was legendary. Her educational approach engaged students to create new ideas, and to place these in dialogue with the theory presented. Prompting the power of each student's imagination, rooted in a genuine love for them, was at the core of her professional work, and provided a base for her own subsequent theory, much of which is represented in these pages.

She would not tolerate misbehaviour in lectures, however, and one stern glance in the silence of a pause quelled the disrespect. Often the offenders later appeared at her door for support and counsel. They knew they were welcome, regardless. I have lost count of the number of letters and times being stopped by former students on Dublin streetscapes subsequent to her passing in 2017, to describe how she influenced their own approach to the teaching of and love for their students. Perhaps this has something to do with why Dr Brian MacCraith, the (former) President of Dublin City University (which now incorporates St Patrick's College) has named a lecture theatre after Dr Gilligan to honour and to remember her.

When Ann Louise returned from Boston College to Dublin in 1983, with myself in clandestine tow as her life-partner, we were both deeply concerned about the number of adults, especially women, who could not access higher education because of growing up in socially and economically underserved communities. So we founded, along with a small group of women, The Shanty Educational Project, named after our home, 'The Shanty', where classes took place for the first fifteen years, not far from the communities of Tallaght West. It was extraordinary to witness her teaching women from these communities – many of whom had not finished second level education – the history of the philosophy of the imagination and the feminist theory of sexual difference. It literally changed their lives, and opened up new ways of their being in the world. This, of course, was not all she taught! And others joined us to offer a range of courses so that participants would have a 'second chance' to be educated and to move into employment and leadership opportunities. Ann Louise refers to this 'practice of love' often throughout this book.

Thirty-five years on, the educational organisation, now known as An Cosán, and located in the heart of Tallaght West, has contributed significantly to the eradication of intergenerational poverty due to the leadership and participation of thousands of others from inside and outside these communities. From a systemic perspective, what is of equal import is how Ann Louise's leadership promoted this type of learning as a new form of higher education, to be recognised and valued by the State. While it was originally known as 'adult education classes in the informal sector', with little state investment, she encouraged state officials to see it as 'community education' with a unique approach towards ensuring the educational success of people coming from a background of poverty or social inequality. When she was appointed by the Minister for Education to the first Board of the independent state agency, Quality and Qualifications Ireland (QQI), it was a prime mission of hers to get the agency to recognise community education as a formal type of higher education. This now has come to pass.

During her last years at St Patrick's College, between 2000 and 2003, Ann Louise established and directed its Educational Disadvantage Centre. Both her work in St Pat's and the communities of Tallaght West prompted a vision for teacher education to include a unique focus on teaching and learning in communities of disadvantage. Under the present leadership of her friend and colleague, Dr Paul Downes, the Centre has expanded its research and teaching programme so that this focus has been mainstreamed into the curriculum and wider work of the university. Together they co-edited a collection of essays,[4] written by educational experts, many of whom are Ann Louise's former students, to offer foundational theories to sustain this work.

After she wrote this book, we began to 'image the possible' for our own lives. We saw on the horizon an Ireland wherein everyone could marry the person they choose to love. We married in Vancouver, British Columbia on

4 *Beyond Educational Disadvantage* (Dublin: IPA, 2007).

13 September 2003. It was a crisp, gloriously sunny fall day. We came home to Ireland soon after and sought to register our marriage just like any other couple who had married outside the state. 'No!' said the State and thus began our preparations for the High and Supreme Court case *Zappone and Gilligan vs. the Revenue Commissioners, Ireland and the Attorney General*, 2006. The case and our public story became the catalyst for the marriage equality movement in Ireland.[5] And on another gloriously sunny day, in May of 2015, Ireland became the first country in the world to say yes to marriage equality through the vote of its people.

Ann Louise did submit this manuscript, upon its completion, to several publishers in Ireland and the USA. No one was willing to publish it. It was one of her greatest professional disappointments. And now, through the generosity of her friend Dr Downes who read it after her passing and thought we should give publishing it one more try (!), and due to the openness of Tony Mason of Peter Lang to take the risk of publishing a 20-year-old manuscript, this beautifully written, profound and impactful work is seeing the light.

As I re-read the manuscript myself so many years later, I was struck by three things. Firstly, as I have mentioned already, Ann Louise was a woman way ahead of her time. The book's relevance, and indeed its necessity in the present, twenty years on, is striking. I shall say more about that momentarily. Secondly, it is *the* philosophic basis upon which she lived her own life and this enabled her capacity to bring about significant individual, social and systemic change with others, time and again. Thirdly, I think it provides us, then, with a philosophic and educational methodology that can continue to enable many of the changes we need today. I tell parts of her story, as I do above, to offer narrative evidence that this is the case.

I hope I have begun to answer the question, 'who was Ann Louise Gilligan?' so that this book has a biographical context for its author. I also want to offer some reflection on its theoretical context, and in so doing, point towards its ongoing relevance and power.[6]

5 See our memoirs for greater detail of this period, and of our educational work in Shanty/An Cosan, *Our Lives Out Loud: In Pursuit of Justice and Equality* (Dublin: O'Brien Press, 2008).

6 I am grateful for conversations with Sarah Murphy and Rebeca Sandu, women of the current generation who each read the full manuscript in full, to help me with this task.

Ann Louise invites the reader to take a journey into feminist theory of the late twentieth century. Equally, it is an invitation – to women and to men – to apply these insights to their own unfolding gender identities through an imagination no longer hindered by patriarchal characteristics and restrictions. She focuses particularly on the need for the becoming of female subjectivity. That women ought to unleash new imaginings to free themselves at their core, thereby laying the groundwork for non-patriarchal mutual relations between women and men.

She shows us how women have begun to do this, and how they reach for new language, cultural and artistic expression to bring female subjectivity into the public domain, as a necessary requirement not only for their own freedom but to support genuine mutual relations between women and men.

While her summons to the reader is very challenging, the tone of her writing style – much like her way of teaching, personal conversation and public oration – gently persuades and never excludes. There are at least two reasons for this, I think. Her theory, and the way she utilises the analytic lens and content of imagination philosophy to create it, is rooted firstly in her own life-long reclaim of the secret of loving relations. She loved herself, fiercely. She loved others, especially those who were most different from her. And through her social activism and practice of silent times, she imagined and loved plurality in the divine.

Secondly, she knew that if people, especially, though not only, women, discovered ways to image the possible for themselves and our world, through doing the hard work of becoming subject, not object of any other, such agency would necessarily change even the most intransigent social, economic and cultural problems to shift violence towards peace, lies towards truth, poverty and inequality towards the flourishing of every one. She bore witness to this in her own life, and in our lives with others.

How does the concept of 'sexual difference', especially as articulated by Luce Irigaray, still hold power for today? We have had the #metoo global movement, in Ireland we witnessed 'Waking the Feminists' as a resistance to male-dominated cultural public showings (originating in a response to the National Theatre's centenary calendar of events). Really, the work of female subjectivity is still in its early stages I would propose. For example, social media is rampant with invitations to boy and girl children to violate and abuse each other, especially girls. Comprehensive sexual education is still in its infancy in many countries, not allowed into the education mainstream, including Ireland. Most countries do not have equal social relations between genders, nor equal representation in the public life of legal and policy decision-making, and of governing.

While it is true that laws and policies must change to continue to forge relations of equality and mutuality, these will only be devised and supported in an effective way by those who are willing to do the hard personal work of becoming subject, finding one's interpersonal and public voice, especially women. We do not have enough of this yet. This is my experience after a decade of public, political life as a Senator and Government Minister in a prosperous, free Western European country.

Furthermore, what about the prising open of the gender and sexual identity spectrum, the rising up in practice, relations and theory of the plurality and diversity of LGBTQ+ people, and non-binary individuals? What about the subjective becoming of every race and ethnic people and how the intersections of identity can be a source of further freedom rather than markers of oppression?

These are prime questions for the twenty-first century – and I think that the ethics of 'dreaming love', as Ann Louise outlines in the final chapter, can and should be applied to the flourishing of every form of identity difference and to the forging of a plurality of new social relations. New language, social and cultural practices, laws and policies will emerge to bring us forward.

But how can we make sure that even some of this happens? As Ann Louise herself says within these pages and I will leave the last words of this foreword to her:

> Our hope for a new future lies in an imagination rooted in love.

New York City, October 2020

Introduction

The interests which developed into this book were born in the mid-70s when I was studying for my Master's degree in Paris. During those two years, I began reading the works of Paul Ricoeur and became convinced that imagination must be reinstated at a philosophical and political level if real change was ever to be realised. During that same period, Luce Irigaray was writing *Speculum de l'Autre Femme*. Our paths did not cross but in my two years of work with psychoanalyst Nadine Durand I became aware of some of the issues I was later to read in Irigaray's work.

My doctoral studies in Boston College during the 1980s allowed me to expand and develop my understanding of the philosophy of the imagination, especially in the works of Paul Ricoeur. With a growing feminist consciousness, I recognised the academic challenge to place a philosophy of imagination in dialogue with feminist theory. Within this interdisciplinary conversation I became convinced that the aspiration for social transformation at the heart of feminist theory would never be concretised unless imagination is accepted as the faculty which could empower new ways of being and of understanding our world.

During the 1990s I have been persuaded that sexual difference is the issue of our age.

To establish a new world order and to survive the chaos of our present plight, sexual difference must be addressed and resolved. Luce Irigaray sees this as an ontological issue: something related to the order of human being and becoming. In other words, what Ricoeur claims for imagination, Irigaray associates with sexual difference.

The practice of sexual difference is a call to live love in a new way. It is a challenge to relate mutually, respecting the other as other, recognising difference, honouring boundaries and yet loving passionately and sensually from a new acceptance of the centrality of our embodiment, our sexuality.

What may sound like a utopian ideal can, I believe, be realised in the concrete struggle of our daily existence by placing in critical and creative interplay the three ideas of imagination, sexual difference and love. This is the task of this book. In the emerging tapestry of the following chapters, the web of possibility which flows from the interconnection of these ideas will become evident.

In the first chapter, I demonstrate how the male imagination has shaped present reality and has been the scaffolding upholding a society of male dominance. In questioning the normativity, the objectivity of the many cultural givens which are the fruit of a male imagination, I call for a relativisation of this perspective and a radical critique of the false imagery of women which has insidiously pervaded our worldview. Within this exposition I show how a male imagination, with its fixity on oneness and sameness, has objectified women. Such objectification is clearly evidenced in the social construction of gender. I indicate further how the oppressive understandings of gender have been fostered and promoted by various religious traditions.

The time has come for women to unravel this legacy and to refuse to be a construct of the male imagination. If women are to become subjects of their own existence, they must break from the fantasy of the male imagination and represent their own specificity – their own difference. To move towards freedom, to reinvent their own subjectivity, women must reclaim their own imaginations in order to shape a new self-image. Claiming the notion of sexual difference is one of the more hopeful political strategies for women as they journey beyond imprisonment in patriarchal projections.

One of the central factors in suppressing female subjectivity and sustaining the monoreality of male existence has been the use of language. In Chapter Two, I show how the discourse that dominates our lives represents a male imagination and ensures that the monologic of maleness remains unquestioned. I also identify the importance of raising critical awareness about the role that religious language has played and continues to play in promoting male dominance and in rendering women silent. If the metamorphosis of consciousness which occurs through the acceptance of sexual difference is to be fully realised, then we must undertake a systematic and intentional analysis of the social structure of language. A feminist analysis of language challenges us to expose imaginatively the false image of permanency which sustains present structures. Such work will allow us to recognise that male language is simply a historical construct riding the river of time and, therefore, can and must be changed. The way forward is to discover a space for the female imagination to come to public expression in language.

As women have been the ones excluded from symbolic representation in the system of sameness, then it must be women who will create a new symbolic expression. Within this chapter I offer some examples of a feminist imagination expressed through a language which reflects female subjectivity. Such breaking open of language to represent sexual difference offers a new perspective on reality and is vital in our search for a world of mutual exchange.

In Chapter Three, I examine the question of divine difference. I show that while maleness has been affirmed in inherited God-language, femaleness has been suppressed, thus silencing a whole aspect of Divine being. Giving voice to a feminist understanding of sexual difference will allow us to grasp new aspects of divinity and will allow us realise that what has been given 'can always be reimagined'.

I indicate that the task of naming and imagining divinity in different ways is vital for the construction of a new society. The way we image the divine is not a benign or neutral force, rather it powerfully impacts the way a society views and structures itself. Exclusive male God-language offers a seal of approval to the normativity of the male human being. If the churches wish to promote a world of equivalence and mutuality then they must insist on a radical rewrite of the theological anthropology which underpins their present teaching.

To speak of the divine is an imaginative act. The heritage of male imagery for the divine reflects a history of men trusting their imaginations and imaging a male divine presence ever calling them forward, ever stretching their potential. The time has come for women to place their experience of difference at the centre of the inquiry for new divine imagery. Within this chapter I explore divine metaphors erupting from the female experiences of sexual difference. As these symbolic representations of the divine enter the public arena, they will necessarily call us to reimage traditional interpretations of the divine as love.

This brings me to the heart of my task. If the insights of feminism related to subjectivity, language and divinity are to mould a practice radical enough to change our world, imagination is the key. In Chapter Four, I hail imagination as a vital faculty, which shapes the way we think about reality and influences the kinds of choices we make. In other words, imagination is at the heart of who we are and what we will become. I examine two questions: how can we articulate an integrated philosophy of the imagination? and, how is our understanding of this faculty of the human person affected by the insights of feminism? The answers begin to emerge through an exposition of the 'pre-historic' imagination and a feminist analysis of the philosophical history of imagination. This, however, is not enough. The historical examination makes no mention of the female imagination. So, I turn to the writings of Luce Irigaray to assist us in developing an understanding of what she calls the female imaginaire. Here we see that an acknowledgement of the reality of sexual difference provides the essential starting point for the birth of a female imagination. I argue that such an analysis and relativisation of the male imagination, and the heralding of the birth of the female imagination, are key building blocks for the feminist imagination. Imagination shot through with feminism will open up entirely new ways of imaging humanity and divinity and will expand our notion of love.

In the fifth and final chapter, I suggest that the promise and prophecy of a feminist imagination remains unfulfilled until it is historically realised, practically concretised. The feminist imagination must impel us towards ethical activities that create a culture of love and social structures that foster a love of difference. I consider some of the ingredients that enable us to dream and act towards such love by identifying foundational concerns for the feminist ethical imagination. In the last section of the chapter, I develop a feminist ethics of love, arguing that this is an appropriate model to hold together the female and male imaginations.

This text is grounded in the particularity of my Irishness. It is also influenced by my social location as a middle-class woman. However, the perspective which accompanies such privilege has been radically altered by a life lived in partnership with women and men who struggle on low incomes in areas of great social disadvantage. Eradicating the injustice of poverty has been a central passion of my existence. I write above all as an Irish feminist. I recognise that this word means different things to different people.

Put otherwise, feminism is not one simple reality. In my life, feminism is a personal and political stance, calling for untiring commitment to the liberation of all women from oppression in its various forms so that full female subjectivity can flourish. Feminism, in my understanding, is a radical critique of structures and systems that block women's power and silence their public participation in shaping society. Feminism is also a creative movement towards the establishment of new images, new representations of women in our world. It is therefore about coupling action for change with deep critical and creative thought as to what such change would look like. Feminism calls each woman to recognise the other woman as other and to struggle together so that each woman's difference is acclaimed. This demands deep sensitivity to and engagement with the issues of class, sexual preference, race and age. Only then can we move forward in sisterhood; only then will justice for women be realised.

Men are not excluded from working towards the ideals of this movement. Indeed, if a world of mutual love is ever to be realised, that is to say, a world rooted in the acceptance of sexual difference, men must resist sexism in all its manifestations and partner in the construction of structures beyond the hierarchies of patriarchy. Therefore, in my understanding of feminism, men are not excluded. However, to be included in the construction of a society where people love mutually and live out their images of sexual difference, most men will have to radically alter their way of being in the world.

I make no claims of hegemony for the following discourse. Rather, I speak humbly of a truth which I have come to see with certain clarity and from within a certain context. As an academic and an activist, as one who has walked the tightrope joining these two worlds for over twenty years, I write as one who knows something of the difficulty and the challenge of this delicate balancing act. However, I am aware that others will write of these same realities in different ways and with different emphases. I would simply aspire that my work would become part of a shared conversation towards the construction of a world of mutual relations, radically committed to love and to imaging the world in new and transformed ways.

CHAPTER ONE

Imagining Female Difference

As each new wave of feminism washes in over the shores of time, the critical question remains: whose image and naming of reality will prevail? Will this present wave simply return to the sea of patriarchy, leaving little changed, or will it alter the coastline of history forever, finally corroding patriarchal representation? The hoped-for permanent transformation from a reality that subjugates women, to a social and cultural order that hails women's different and inherent value, rests with the feminist imagination: an imagination which opens up entirely novel ways of imaging humanity and divinity.

There are two critical and urgent tasks for the feminist imagination with regard to an understanding of being human. First, it must expose the false imagery of the past. Towards this end, I demonstrate in this chapter how the mainstay of male domination is simply a construct of the male imagination. I outline how the 'cultural givens' of male superiority, male normativity and male subjectivity, are not preordained truths but rather gender constructs rooted in an imagination which has been preoccupied with sameness, oneness and fixity. It is essential for the feminist imagination to prise open cultural values in which the assertion of some humans is dependent on the subordination and suppression of others. The time is ripe to break with 'the economy of the same' and allow difference, especially women's difference, to shimmer forth.

The second, and far more difficult undertaking, is to explore the question of how women can move from this inherited imagery and courageously come to be their authentic selves. What tools can women use in order to get in touch with their own subjectivity as women? What images will assist us in this exploration? How will women loosen the past cultural restrictions of their imaginations in order to freely picture a new way of being and knowing? Throughout this chapter, my interest is in proposing a worldview where relations of mutual sustainment between women, between men, and between women and men, can flourish. Such potential to live mutual lives of loving relatedness is also dependent on a spirituality that sustains and nourishes this way of being human.

Exposing False Imagery

The symbolic devaluing of women is one of the founding metaphors of Western civilisation. Within the framework of early Greek philosophy (fourth century BCE), reality was understood hierarchically and imaged in dualisms. The male rational world was elevated as having the potential to image the divine, while the female affective world – rooted in nature – was deemed defective in this regard. Within this schema imagination was viewed as a lesser faculty than reason, something to be feared and suppressed. The residual effects of this worldview have seeped through time and continue to shape the imagination of twentieth-century living.

This dualistic worldview is clearly imaged in the construction of gender: the cultural creation of male and female roles. What we have inherited as the way things are, is in fact the representation of women by men. The familiar stereotypes of woman as 'other', as 'closer to nature', as 'passive', simply serve to reinforce the image of male dominance.[1] This objectification of women continues to pervade the media, especially the

1 In her most recent book. *Making Gender: The Politics and Erotics of Culture* (Boston: Beacon Press, 19%) Sherry B. Ortner returns to her argument on the causes of women's subordination. In 1972 she published the groundbreaking essay 'Is Female to Male as Nature is to Culture'. Now more than two decades on the debate over 'universal' male dominance continues. While a post-modern climate calls in question any universal or absolute claims about the causes of male dominance, and while anthropologists today see 'culture' as a much more complex and disjunctive concept, in Ortner's view the female/nature; male/culture opposition still remains as a widespread (if not universal) structure. See especially chapter 7 of *Making Gender*.

world of advertisement, albeit in subtler forms.[2] I concur with Michele Le Doeuff in her rejection of this state of affairs: 'I strongly object to the use of "woman" as a construct of the imagination.'[3]

The Link between False Imagery and Violence against Women

Pornography and violence against women are a direct result of failing to image the mutual worth of male and female existence. This is why it is so essential to expose the false imagery associated with the construct 'woman'. That which we objectify we can abuse with greater ease than that which we love and relate to mutually. The link between pornography and rape has been written about adequately to confirm the connection. However, in linking imagery and violence against women we must insist on the dissolution of that dualistic distinction between 'hard' and 'soft' pornography. All imagery which objectifies women is insidious and must be rejected.

It is important to note that violent crimes against women are on the increase, that this is a global phenomenon and happens even in Western countries which claim sophisticated equality legislation. Again, the link between imagery that objectifies women and the violation of real women must be critically examined and exposed.[4] As the media continues to portray

2 In October 1996 a survey was conducted in Dublin, Ireland by the members of a Women's Studies Diploma course at the Shanty Educational Project. The women bought the entire range of magazines on sale during that month from a large newsagents. They then analysed each magazine in relation to text and imagery. Their findings unveiled a startling prevalence of sexism and pornography in this wide range of popular reading material.

3 Michele le Doeuff in an interview with Raoul Mortley in *Philosophers in Conversation* (New York: Routledge, 1991), p. 87.

4 Some recent statistics will help to illustrate the point: 'In the United States between two and four thousand women die each year as a direct result of battering' (FBI statistics). Abuse of women happens in about half of all male/female cohabiting relationships (National Clearing House on domestic violence). One in seven women is

images of the ideal, perfect woman or the passive, serving woman, some men cannot cope with relationships in everyday life with strong women who seek to be treated as persons in their own right. Furthermore, as advertisements which objectify women are not rooted in the reality of women's experience, they become quickly jaded and need constant injections of sensationalism in order to grip the consumer's tired imagination. Violence against women is a manifestation of male fear of women, male hatred of women, male need to control women. Such fear and hatred are fed on false imagery. The social construction of gender in our society allows 'many men to understand love as possession and violence as an acceptable means of control'.[5]

False Imagery and the Social Construction of Gender

It is vital to be aware of the fact that the social construction of gender is a historic process – it is not a given, nor a normative absolute. In patriarchal time it has produced a hierarchical way of relating which has shaped history up to our present day. However, the evolution of history can be altered; we can interrupt this oppressive tradition and claim our own power to create new ways of being in relation.

The social construction of gender is shaped by what happens in everyday life.[6] The more women comply with the stereotypical images of the dominant culture, the more we are oiling the wheels of patriarchy. Furthermore, as the given construction of gender constantly informs and shapes women's experience of reality, it will take a deliberate decision by

---

a victim of marital rape. (From *Rape in Marriage* by Diana Russell). These statistics are cited in Rosemary Haughton's book *Song in a Strange Land: The Wellspring Story and the Homelessness of Women* (Illinois: Templegate Publishers, 1991), p. 30.

5 Catherine Keller, *From a Broken Web: Separation, Sexism & Self* (Boston: Beacon Press, 1986).

6 In her article, 'The Invention of French Feminism: An Essential Move.' (*Yale French Studies*, Vol. 1. 1995, Christine Delphy challenges us to recognise that social construction is not the same thing as social conditioning or socialisation. 'There is no "beyond" (or indeed "before") social construction,' p. 204.

women to stand back and critically examine the imagery which surrounds them in order to reject that which fails to represent their own deep sense of who they are and who they wish to become.

The work of Cindy Sherman is particularly helpful in this regard. Sherman, a feminist photographer, has used her work to confront the stereotypes of women's lives. Since her first imaginary 'Film Stills' – a set of eighty black and white self-portraits – she has played with satire and mimicry to challenge women to revisit and re-experience the various roles which society has expected them to fulfil. Each image reveals the complexity, the ambiguity of life lived by women in a man-made world. There is nothing precise or unequivocal about the content of these images. After viewing Sherman's art, one is left with far more questions than answers. One thing is clear however: radical social change begins by altering the patterns of our banal, ordinary, everyday lives. In a later series titled 'Historical Portraits', she revisits the classical tradition of portrait painting. In this set of images, she manages to reveal the emptiness, the hollowness of life lived by the heroes of history.[7] Here again her work is full of irony and parody.

Following on from viewing these slides from Sherman's work, women can be encouraged to engage in what Irigaray calls 'mimesis'. Mimesis or mimicry involves a process of 'playful repetition', whereby women wilfully choose to step into the roles and stereotypes imposed on them by men and from this position erode an insidious grip on their lives. Here is a powerful tool for women to subvert the social order and to open the possibility for social and cultural change.[8]

To play with mimesis is thus, for a woman, to try to recover the place of her exploitation by discourse, without allowing herself to be simply reduced to it. It means to resubmit herself to ideas about herself, that are elaborated either in or by a masculine logic, but to do so to make 'visible', by an effect of playful repetition, what was supposed to remain invisible. It also means to 'unveil' the fact that if women are such good mimics, it is because they are not simply resorbed in this function. They also simultaneously remain

7 Cindy Sherman, *Historical Portraits* (New York: Rizzoli, 1991).

8 Luce Irigaray, *This Sex Which is Not One* (New York: Cornell University, 1985), p.76.

elsewhere. This clever technique is so effective that Irigaray herself names it as 'wicked', 'diabolical'![9] In my own work, I have seen its power in bringing the invisible to visibility, the unconscious to consciousness: a vital step in motivating action towards social and political change. Merleau-Ponty stated that the visible is a 'lining of the invisible', which is to say that the invisible is not the opposite of the visible but its depth.[10]

To dismantle the patriarchal construction of gender will involve exposing the falseness underpinning the polarity created by such terms as 'masculinity' and 'femininity'. To be feminine is not an image which calls woman to her unique self-expression. Rather, it is a negation, a statement of what masculinity is not. Masculinity, on the contrary, calls males to the full expression of patriarchal manhood. The residue, the shadow side of this dominant human being, is packaged as femininity. Another way of speaking about this is to say that femininity is a nothingness, a manipulative image which distracts women from the development of their own subjectivity as they give over their lives to incorporating the negative aspects of patriarchal maleness. Such effort leads to the deterioration and decay of real womanhood. Doris Lessing puts it well:

> They watched their own deterioration like merciless onlookers. These days all over the world there are people like these, mostly women: the states of mind that once only affected people on death-beds or at moments of acute crisis are their permanent condition. Lives that appear to them meaningless, wasted, hang around their backs like decaying carcasses.[11]

The gender construction of masculinity and femininity is clearly a hierarchical and dualistic model. While women are called to be different to men – expressing their feminine side and complementing male masculinity – their difference, their otherness is clearly inferior. She is the 'lack', the inessential aspect of maleness. When measured against the One normative way of being human, being feminine – while titillating the warmth and comfort of private

9 Ibid.

10 This point is elaborated in Susan Kozel's article 'The Diabolical Strategy of Mimesis: Luce Irigaray' Reading of Maurice Merleau-Ponty.' *Hypatia* Vol. II, No. 3. Summer 1996. p. 116.

11 D. Lessing, *Landlocked* (London: MacGibbon & Kee, 1965), p. 212.

existence – is clearly not essential. Furthermore, the myth of the 'Eternal feminine' has a shadow side which is weak, evil and always to be feared.[12] A feminist imagination enables women to reject the notion of femininity by breaking from the victim mentality it creates and by naming it clearly 'as the justificatory apparatus of our subordination'.[13] The consequent imaginative challenge to women is to recapture femaleness from femininity.

The popular counterposition to these images of complementarity – which as I have outlined complement nothing but unbridled maleness – are the images of equality. Within a liberal mindset the answer to sexism is to challenge women to become equal to men. Luce Irigaray's quip, 'to be equal to men is not to be equal at all',[14] cleverly deflates any romanticisation of the notion of equality. Understandings of equality have failed to challenge the fixed androcentric world of male dominance. Women who want equality must stretch and strain to fit into their ambience – must become as males. Demanding equality, as women, seems to me to be an erroneous expression of a real issue. Demanding to be equal presupposes a term of comparison. Equal to what? As Irigaray queries: 'To whom or to what do women want to be equalised? To men? To a salary? To a public office? To what standard? Why not to themselves?'[15] Equality promotes a world of sameness, oneness, where female difference, otherness, is submerged and obliterated. Again Irigaray reminds us: 'We shall die together if you do not let me go outside your sameness.'[16] Women who accept male-imagined notions of equality are in fact 'becoming agents of their own annihilation, reducing themselves to a sameness that is not their own. It becomes a kind of magma, of night in which all they cats are grey, from which man, or humanity, extracts for free what he needs'.[17]

12 In passing it must also be stated that 'traditional masculinity distorts men.' See Adrienne Rich, *What Is Found There: Notebooks on Poetry and Politics* (New York: W. W. Norton & Company, 1993), p. 26.

13 Drucella Cornell, *Beyond Accommodation: Ethical Feminism, Deconstruction and the Law* (New York: Routledge, 1991), p. 10.

14 Luce Irigaray, *Je, Tu, Nous* (New York: Routledge, 1993), p. 12.

15 Ibid., p. 12.

16 Luce Irigaray, *Elemental Passions* (London: Athlone Press, 1992), p. 14.

17 Luce Irigaray, *An Ethics of Sexual Difference* (New York: Cornell University Press, 1993), p. 104.

'Woman' and Religious Imagery

The cultural construction of gender, in its promotion of the image of woman as 'feminine other' of the 'equal same', has been fostered and promoted by various religious traditions. Religious imagery is a powerful force and has a capacity to free-wheel through our lives, evoking memories from the past and startling us in the present with thoughts and feelings which we believe we have long since outgrown. For women to break from a construction of gender which has oppressed their lives and blocked their ability to touch their own subjectivity as self-identified women, it is essential to unravel this legacy.

There is no need here to re-present the research or to redemonstrate the diatribe of demeaning imagery of women that we have inherited from the Church Fathers within the Christian tradition. We are all too familiar with this inheritance which imaged women as 'the devil's gateway, as Eve's co-conspirators'. As Tertullian said: 'You are the devil's gateway … you are she who persuaded him whom the devil did not dare attack … Do you not know that everyone of you is an Eve? The sentence of God on your sex lives on in this age, the guilt of necessity lives on too.'[18] The cacophonous sound of Tertullian's words could be orchestrated with many examples. Clearly, the rejection of woman, imaged as the 'feminine other', is operative here.

In many texts, we also encounter the image of woman striving to be the 'equal same'; strong women needed to deny their gender and become as men in order to be accepted. Mary Condren in her book *The Serpent and the Goddess* tells the story of St Monenna, a fifth-century saint who was in contact with St Brigid and St Patrick: 'She travelled to Rome several times and was paid the dubious compliment of having "a man's spirit in a woman's body".'[19] Women often participated in this oppression by imaging themselves as men in moments of great strength or crisis. The life of Perpetua, a third-century leader in the Church, is a case in point. The day before her

18 Tertullian, *De Cultu Feminarium* 1.12.

19 Mary Condren, *The Serpent and the Goddess: Women, Religion & Power in Celtic Ireland* (San Francisco: Harper & Row, 1989), p. 101.

martyrdom, Perpetua had a vision where she was in the arena awaiting the wild beasts to tear her apart. As she stood fearlessly before her contenders she recalled: 'I was stripped of my clothing and suddenly I was a man.'[20] The immasculinisation of women by men, the striving of women to be like men, is profoundly problematic, especially as one reflects that among the guiding principles of this male world is misogyny.

Our analysis of religious imagery from the tradition of story and text should be paralleled with an examination of an equally important form of discourse, namely, visual imagery. Many insights about women's subordination can be gleaned from a critical evaluation of religious art in all its manifestation. Indeed, the popular religious understanding of a period can often be more adequately gathered by viewing the visual account. Engaging in a hermeneutics of the image in history, Margaret Miles agrees that this heritage is also androcentric, because of course our inheritance of religious art is by and large the production of the male imagination.[21] However, imagery is more expressive of the affective and catches up the respondent in a relationship of feeling that is often absent in the narrative of the word. The image can take on a life of its own as it permeates through history bearing tidings unintended by its originator. Therefore, it is simplistic to condemn as unhelpful to women all visual religious imagery. The least we must concede is that this is an extremely complex inheritance and should be revisited with alertness and caution. Part of this cautionary response will be to note how frequently women are represented in their sexual and reproductive roles as vessels to be filled. Such imagery has been profoundly influential in shaping women's perception of themselves, especially in relation to their sexuality.[22]

20 From 'The Martyrdom of Perpetua: A Protest Account of Third Century Christianity', in *A Lost Tradition: Women Writers of the Early Church*, eds, Patricia Wilson-Kastner et al. (New York: University Press of America, 1981), p. 24.

21 Margaret Miles, *Image as Insight*.

22 For a similar viewpoint see Pat Holden, ed. *Women's Religious Experience* (London: Croom Helm, 1983), see intro, pp. 1–12.

'Woman' and the Postmodernist Imagination

As already indicated, the cultural construction of gender which we have inherited oppresses women, promoting images of woman as 'feminine other' or 'equal same'. While such imagery from the past is still rampant in our societies, there is a new and in a sense even more insidious image coming to birth today within post-modern discourse. As a reaction to the autonomous self-promoted by the Enlightenment, postmodernism speaks of the demise of meaning, the 'death of self'. While such a discourse has positive implications as it pushes us beyond the arrogant absolutes and insular individualism of former times, it must nevertheless be viewed with caution. Women and all subjugated peoples must view with suspicion any philosophical system which announces the demise of self at the very time when the political challenge of feminism is that we as women become who we are. We seem to be denied our subjectivity just as we discover it, or as the black author and activist bell hooks puts it: 'It's easy to give up your identity when you've already got one.'[23] The passage, with unseemly haste, from an order which only recognises male subjectivity, to one which denies any possibility for subjectivity at all, may be viewed quizzically. Is this but a clever ploy to avoid critiquing the absolute ideology of maleness which has ruled our world? Is it but an inversion of male arrogance and a further means of silencing women? Feminists must firmly refuse the postmodernist disavowal of identity. In fact, within the feminist imagination 'the subject returns from its dispersal and disappearance … to raise the political, historical and social question of subjectivity'.[24]

This said, it must be recognised that the search for a self in the fluidity, plurality and relativity that marks our era will make self-assertion for women an ever more challenging but necessary task. I join with Julia

23 As quoted by Anne Seller in 'Whose Knowledge? Whose Post-Modernism' in *Women's Philosophy Review* No. 11, 1994, p. 48.

24 Marianne Hirsch, *The Mother-Daughter Plot: Narrative, Psychoanalysis, Feminism* (Bloomington: Indiana University Press, 1989), p. 139.

Kristeva when she 'speaks in favour of imagination as antidote for the crisis'.[25] The challenge for women of making the transition from 'feminine other' or 'equal same' to self-defined, 'mutual other' is well portrayed in Marge Piercy's poem 'Unlearning Not to Speak'.[26] Here a woman is invited to learn to speak again, beginning with her own I, (or We), her own hunger, pleasure and rage.

Moving beyond the Male-Imagined Woman

The challenge to move from critique to creative construction is above all a challenge to the feminist imagination, a challenge to image the 'I', the 'we' that is born in female subjectivity. The feminist imagination summons women to 'theorise the terms on which the female imaginary can assume an identity and not be colonised by the male … we must create our own space in the symbolic order'.[27] If women are to become subjects of their existence, they must break from the fantasy of the male imagination and represent themselves as different – yes – but different above all to the male perception of what that difference might be. The goal, Irigaray reminds us, is 'to be really two sexes each with its own imaginary and its own order'.[28] The female imagination, an imagination which has been suppressed until now, will be the site for the birth of women's subjectivity. Irigaray prophesies: 'Then the "same" would repossess its "other", leaving the "other woman" free to signify her own division, her own "same" and her own "other"'.[29]

25 Julia Kristeva, *Tales of Love* (New York: Columbia University Press, 1987), p. 381.

26 Marge Piercy, *Circles on the Water* (New York: Alfred A. Knopf, 1986), p. 97.

27 Caroline Williams, 'Feminism, Subjectivity and Psychoanalysis: Towards a (Corpo) real Knowledge', in *Knowing the Difference: Feminist Perspectives in Epistemology*, ed. Kathleen Lennon & Margaret Whitford (London: Routledge, 1994), p. 174.

28 Luce Irigaray, *The Irigaray Reader*, ed. Margaret Whitford (Oxford: Basil Blackwell Ltd, 1991), p. 87.

29 Luce Irigaray as quoted by Margaret Whitford in *Philosophy in the Feminine* (London: Routledge, 1991), p. 187.

In this claiming of self-definition, an identity women can call their own, the givens of cultural construction will crack and strain and profound change will result. Here we are not tinkering with transformation but radically upending what has been comfortably accepted as the only way of being. When women become subjects in their own right, they too will become, as Luce Irigaray argues, 'producers of scientific, philosophical, religious and political truth'.[30] Present existence is predicated on the mirror images of woman as being non-man, lesser-man or equal-man. To posit female subjectivity is to crack the mirror of sameness and allow us to reflect the multiplicity, the rich diversity that marks human being and human becoming.

How can women express subjectivity as two, not one; claim identity as different, not same? We must search the margins of language and push the boundaries of patriarchal expression in order to find an imaginative excess that could render the richness of female subjectivity. Rosi Braidotti, feminist philosopher, writing from this new space and time, 'has a vision of the thinking, knowing subject as not-one but rather as being split over and over again in a rainbow of yet uncoded and ever so beautiful possibilities'.[31] In other words, 'the beautiful possibilities' which will unfold as women lisp their identity will be marked by a fluidity, a multiplicity and an openness that is ever new.

Re-imagining 'Woman': Sexual Difference

What image, what symbol can best assist this new construction of gender where female and male subjectivity are given voice in mutual harmony? Luce Irigaray has no hesitancy in responding: 'The most obvious symbol, that closest to hand and also most easily forgotten, is the living symbol

30 Luce Irigaray, *An Ethics of Sexual Difference* (New York: Cornell University Press, 1993), p. 121.

31 Rosi Braidotti, 'The Politics of Ontological Difference', in Theresa Brennan, *Between Feminism and Psychoanalysis* (London: Routledge, 1989), p. 101.

of sexual difference.'[32] She adds: 'Women's exploitation is based on sexual difference; its solution will only come through sexual difference.'[33] Irigaray speaks of sexual difference in a variety of ways, as a symbol, as a concept, as an ethics and as a practice. The practice of sexual difference seeks to shatter the sameness of how human nature has been imaged up until now. In the mirror of patriarchy we've grown accustomed to the face of maleness as the only face that is given public representation in our society. The politics of sexual difference calls us to image the differences, the asymmetry, which exists between the sexes. On the other hand this is not a reversion to biological essentialism, which simply recognised the biological differences between the sexes. Biological essentialism only allowed the male sex to break its links with nature and take its place as a subject free to shape culture. The practice of sexual difference as proposed by Irigaray challenges both women and men to live into their own unique subjectivities and to give expression to the richly creative diversity that could shape our world. In other words, taking the symbol of sexual difference seriously is an integral dimension to any new framework which hopes to support mutual relations. This notion, which is central to the works of Luce Irigaray, acts as a fulcrum for women, empowering them to name and to claim their difference. Furthermore, as Gail Grossman Freyne correctly argues, it 'encourages the creation of an identity which hasn't simply been repressed up until now, but which has never been represented at all'.[34]

Although recognising the chequered history that has accompanied the construct of sexual difference and cognisant of the complexities of the current debate, I stand with Irigaray in claiming this term as it has the power to transform perspective. It will radically alter the way we view reality. As early as 1959, the philosopher Edith Stein asked us to reflect on the 'double syntax' of human nature:

32 Luce Irigaray, *An Ethics of Sexual Difference*, p. 113.

33 Irigaray, *Je, Tu, Nous*, p. 12.

34 Gail Grossman Freyne, *From Equal Object to Different Subject: The Quest for Women's Identity Within Marriage* (MA thesis in Women's Studies, UCD, 1994), p. 50.

> I am convinced that the species human being reveals itself to be a double species, man and woman, that the essence of the human being – from which no essential characteristic can be missing – is imprinted by this duality, and that its entire structure bears this specific stamp. It is not just a matter of [male and female] bodies being differently constructed, it is not just individual physiological functions that are different, rather the entire physical life is different, the relationship between body and soul is different, and with the soul the relationship between spirit and the senses is different, as are the relationships among the various spiritual powers.[35]

Imaging Female Difference

To claim women's difference from men is certainly not to claim a bland sameness among women themselves. On the contrary, the notion of difference encourages each woman to recognise the differences within herself and to respect the rich variety of difference between and among women. As Rosi Braidotti states, 'each real-life woman is a multiplicity in herself: split, fractured, a network of levels of experience'.[36] Recognising the differences within difference releases the symbol of sexual difference from the judgement and accusation of essentialism." In promoting the notion of sexual difference, we are not engaging in an archaeological dig to try to discover 'woman's essential nature'. Rather, we are recognising that to transform the cultural valuations of gender which we have inherited and which are oppressive of women, we must create a theory of gender which is sexed. This is the challenge to become 'post-woman' women."[37] In other words, we are born female, but then we inherit patriarchal representations of what is means to be 'woman'; so therefore we must become women.

35 Edith Stein, *The Problems of Women's Education*, Edith Stein's Werke, Vol. 5. Louvain Nauwelaerts & Freiburg: Herder, 1959, p. 138. While Stein and Irigaray would disagree on the ontological and theological grounds for their claims, they both consistently claim difference as a key and liberative concept.

36 Rosi Braidotti, *Nomadic Subjects* (New York: Columbia University Press, 1993), p. 15.

37 Rosi Braidotti, as quoted by Gail Freyne, p. 66.

If the feminist imagination is the site for the birth of women's subjectivity and if sexual difference is the symbol which will act as a fulcrum towards female becoming, how can we empower women to claim their identity in the concreteness of ordinary existence? Another way of asking this question is: how can we move the insights of feminist theory on gender and difference into the practice of everyday life?

Women Recreating Themselves with Each Other

Susan Griffin answers the above question by calling on women 'to create a culture within a culture'. It is vital that women create space and time, places and contexts in which they can be together, and can encourage each other to recreate themselves. Women need to meet and give meaning to their experiences which otherwise could remain, in the words of Hanna Arendt: 'An unbearable sequence of sheer happenings.' In giving voice to her experience, a women can move an experience from the realm of the privatised brute fact, to a public statement which could now shape her own subjectivity, her own sense of self. To engage the narrative of her own life is vital in shaping an understanding of her own identity. This is particularly true as one observes the power of one narrative to empower other women within the group to share their experiences and to live into the truth of their lives. As women we have a deep intuition that we are different and that we experience reality differently. Yet it is only when these experiences are shared and affirmed with each other that women find courage to claim their own voice. Anne Setter remarks: 'It's not so much that we (as women) are aware of different things, but that we are aware of the same things differently.'[38] The healing nature of conversation conducted systematically allows women to touch into their own particularity, their own difference, and to affirm each other in the tentative

38 Anne Setter, 'Realism versus Relativism: Towards a Politically Adequate Epistemology' in *Feminist Perspectives in Philosophy*, eds, Morwenna Griffiths and Margaret Whitford (Indianapolis: Indiana University Press, 1988), p. 177.

process of becoming a self. As Kearney reminds us: 'The shortest route from the self to itself is through the images of others.'[39] We come to our identity in relationship with other women.

To believe that women's experience is distinctive and worthy of attention is something that women themselves must be the first to claim. For women to name their experiences, and ultimately their own identity, they must peel back layers of false imagery imposed upon them by patriarchal projection and then gradually construct their own self-image, one which reflects their experience of becoming women. As Nelle Morton states so accurately: 'Deep in the experience itself is the source of new imagining.'[40] In other words, if we touch into and take the particularity of our experiences seriously, we will find new ways of imaging humanity and divinity; new understandings of what is real.

Healing Painful Imagery

One of the best ways of developing women's critical awareness about images and metaphors that bind and oppress, and images that open up and liberate, is to encourage them to work in small groups within an educational setting of warmth, beauty and care. Good facilitation can encourage the sharing of stories which can spark the imagination and gradually lead to awareness. Such work is process of raising both consciousness and unconsciousness:

> I heard stories about battered women for months before something odd and eerie happened. I saw flickering and confused images in the back of my mind, images of my father picking up a butcher knife and going after my mother … her

39 Richard Kearney, *Poetics of Imagining*: From Husserl to Lyotard (London: HarperCollins Academic, 1991), p. 141.

40 Morton, 'Beloved Image' in *The Journey is Home* (Boston: Beacon Press, 1985), p. 127.

> picking up a frying pan to fend him off ... him with a baseball bat ... her running away.[41]

To take space to allow the eruption of such negative imagery within a 'holding' environment can open up the possibility of healing which is only feasible when the boil is lanced and the poison released. To rid the world of violence without we must deal with the violence within and cleanse our psyches of destructive imagery. Complete healing from the trauma of violence and abuse is possible but only when the healing journey involves a spiritual dimension.

As women we can no longer permit the process of obfuscation or suppression of imagery that oppresses us. Exposing and resisting such imagery will not be welcomed by the systems of domination which are supported by its presence. The dominant ideology always assumes the right to image and to define reality and this leads to imaging the non-dominant as an object to be controlled. It is unrealistic to expect that those who hold the power to image and shape society would name the lie of imagination which informs their worldview. Rather, our efforts must be to raise critical awareness among those who are victims of such imagery.

> This above all, to refuse to be a victim. Unless I can do that I can do nothing, I have to recant, give up the old belief that I am powerless and because of it nothing I will do will ever hurt anyone ... Withdrawal is no longer possible and the alternative is death.[42]

Women's Subjectivity and Interconnectivity

The movement from silent victim to speaking subject can best be realised through female interconnectivity. Here it is evidenced that any movement towards a new subjectivity for women takes place within an

41 Mary Pellauer, 'Moral Callousness and Moral Sensitivity: Violence Against Women', in *Women's Consciousness; Women's Conscience,* eds, Barbara Hilkert Andolsen et al. (Minneapolis: Winston Press, 1985), pp. 34–35.

42 Margaret Attwood, *Surfacing* (New York: Popular Library', 1972), pp. 222–223.

intersubjective setting. As Rosi Braidotti poetically reminds us: 'The new subjectivity will be one of interconnected nomadism.'[43] Any progression through the particularity of each woman's experience towards a new identity, happens within the environment of a loving community. The self comes into existence within a relational context. The separate self staunchly defended by the phallic worldview is dissolved in the rainbow of interconnected, diversely complex, richly fluid, sharings of women's togetherness. Furthermore, each self is no longer imaged as fixed and separate but rather as multi-layered and in constant flux: 'The self is a sort of network of interrelated points.'[44]

Catherine Keller, writing on the place of connectivity as integral to female becoming, states: 'The relational self is bound up with the "female" in only one important way: women are less likely, under the conditions of patriarchy, to have repressed the fluidity and connectivity of which all persons consist. The awareness of the fluent sociality of ourselves is more likely to have been incorporated into the very structure of our personality, reinforcing rather than repressing connective sensibilities.'[45] Thus I would claim that the possibilities for female becoming can best be realised within the climate of interconnectivity. The sense of a connected self can also be developed through dialogue with images of women deposited in history. The autonomous self of the male world gives way to a sense of identity based in culture, stretching back and forth through time.[46] Viewing images from times past, reading historical voices of women's lives, can spark new insight into an as yet unspoken world.

This process of interconnectivity is not always easy. It demands listening to the most marginal amongst us and hearing their experience to the point that we are changed to the depths of our own becoming.[47] The act of recognising herself as an/other in her own right a woman, will hopefully

43 Rosi Braidotti, *Patterns of Dissonance*, p. 281.

44 Roisi Braidotti, *Nomadic Subjects*, p. 31.

45 Keller, *From a Broken Web: Separation, Sexism, and Self* (Boston: Beacon Press, 1985), p. 127.

46 An excellent resource of images of women from Irish history is published by.

47 This point is elaborated in Morwenna Griffiths, *Feminism and the Self: The Web of Identity* (London: Routledge 1995).

open her to those around her, without any need to order the differences she encounters into hierarchical strata.

Women's Subjectivity and Imagination

I would posit that the imagination is central to create women's subjectivity, if that which is possible, is to be. In the painful work of change and transformation, in letting go of much that offered security (however false), women shift from perceiving imagination and imagery as benign and neutral to acknowledging this faculty for its powerful ability to name, shape and image reality. The veil is lifted and imagination is recognised as so deeply embedded in our natures 'that it more than anything else controls our lives.'[48] If we as women have been imprisoned in patriarchal projections of who we ought to be, the only way to move towards freedom, to reinvent our own subjectivity, is to reclaim our own imagination in order to shape our own self-image. Changing our self-image will lead quickly to acting differently in the world. Put otherwise, the process of deconstruction must gradually give way to creative reconstruction, a process also captured by Adrienne Rich in her poem 'Planetarium'. [49]

To begin to reconstitute our lives as women, to reclaim our identity, is to proclaim a new understanding of rationality. Rationality now holds intellect, emotion and imagination in a mutual embrace. The dichotomised practice of relegating feeling and imagination, as lesser faculties, to the private sphere of living, is no longer acceptable. Allowing imagination to be the midwife in women's rebirth opens up the layers of complexity within our experience, and allows us recognise that there is always more to experience and more in what we experience than we can predict.[50] The

48 James Engel, *The Creative Imagination: Enlightenment to Romanticism* (Boston, MA: Harvard University Press, 1981), p. 52.

49 Adrienne Rich from *The Fact of a Doorframe: Poems Selected and New 1950–1984* (New York: W.W. Norton & Company, 1984), p. 116.

50 Mary Warnock in her classic text titled *Imagination* makes this link between imagination and experience (London: Faber & Faber, 1976) p. 203.

best way to be imaginative is to act imaginatively. The most effective way to develop our own creative capacities is to dive deep and touch the depths of our own experience as women: to take time and space to be creative.

Such exercise of imagination opens up a voyage of rediscovery of women's true selves. Such creative sharing encourages a radical truthfulness and unveils the lie of imagination which we have bathed in for so long. Then:

> As women share experiences … a terror of rediscovery seizes them in that they discover behind inculcated modes of behaviour which have now become questionable a psychological world of their wishes and dreams which has always existed. Anyone who enters it self-critically, lovingly and with patience can discover this archetypal world of wholeness and totality.[51]

Whether as Carol Christ claims here women's becoming is a process of rediscovery or whether as Luce Irigaray claims it is a process of invention, a coming into being of that which does not yet exist, or whether it is both, is open to conversation. But what is clear is that if women are to be empowered to claim their difference, to speak from the place of their own subjectivity, then imagination is the key. This claiming of subjectivity is captured eloquently in May Sarton's poem, 'Now I Become Myself'.[52] Here the poet's creative journey as a woman brings her life and work together in the making of this poem, which allows her to stand still, rooted in love.

Women's Subjectivity and the Sacred

As women journey towards full womanhood by exploring and naming the depths of their own experience and as they challenge the world of imagery to reflect the reality of their lives, they must enter the womb of their

51 Carol P. Christ, *Laughter of Aphrodite: Reflections on a Journey to the Goddess* (San Francisco: Harper & Row, 1987).

52 From *Collected Poems 1930–1993* (New York: W.W. Norton, 1993), p. 162.

imaginations and bring to birth images of the sacred, insights into the holy, which resonate with our own divine potential. Katherine Zappone reminds us that 'the feminist spiritual journey happens in the presence of the Sacred. This presence – expressed through myriad images, metaphors, and concepts – enables the movement of holiness'.[53]

Integral to women's subjectivity, towards the reinvention of identity, is the challenge to rechart, reimage our relation to divinity. Women's journey to the source of their experience must be a journey which allows long periods of stillness and meditative quiet. Recognising the oppression of negated selfhood must lead to periods of silent self-awareness, as well as exercises of political action. Adrienne Rich charts a similar journey in her poem 'The Images' where a woman's presence to her deep self enables a re-membering and recollection.[54]

Conclusion

It is clear, therefore, that women's search for a new identity, a subjectivity rooted in the acceptance of sexual difference, will not be realised at the level of rational reflection alone or disembodied discourse. Neither will insight into new patterns of mutual relation between women and men be gained simply at a theoretical level. Rather, whispers of possible solutions call us to trust our creative selves. Exercising a feminist imagination, an imagination rooted in an integration of body, emotion, mind and spirit will open up imagery which, if acted upon, will realise an extraordinary world. Within the Appendices to this chapter I give two examples from a selection of exercises which I have developed with women and which have proved exciting in flexing and developing our feminist creative imaginations. This work is vital if the current wave of feminism is to swell

53 Katherine Zappone, *The Hope for Wholeness: A Spirituality for Feminists* (Mystic, CT: Twenty-Third Publications, 1991), p. 165.

54 Adrienne Rich, *A Wild Patience Has Taken Me Thus Far*. Poems 1978–1981 (New York: W.W. Norton & Co. 1981), p. 5.

the tide of life lived in harmony, respecting difference and empowering the potential of all. 'The challenge today is to find new images of thought to help feminists think about changes and changing conditions that they have contributed to bring about.'[55] This is the work of the feminist imagination.

55 Rosi Braidotti, *Nomadic Subjects*, p. 276.

CHAPTER TWO

The Social Analysis of Language: Imagining a New Symbolic

> That it is not the literal past, the 'facts' of history, that shape us, but the images of the past embodied in language.
>
> *Brian Friel*[1]

Imagination is the hinge which opens the possibility for the critical recomposition of women's individual and shared experiences. However, as women delve to explore the caverns of their different experiences, a common problem surfaces, namely, the failure of male language to encode and express female subjectivity. It becomes quickly evident that if the metamorphosis of consciousness which occurs through the acceptance of sexual difference is to be fully realised, then we must undertake a systematic and intentional social analysis, especially in relation to language. The acknowledgement of sexual difference has the potential to alter radically the social order. This is only possible, however, if the social structure of language breaks from its monoreality of the male imagination and encompasses the words born of the experience of femaleness and difference. This requires an analysis undertaken from a feminist perspective that will open the way for systemic change by exposing the interlacing of structures and institutions which continue to oppress women. In other words, individual awareness of monologic and monolanguage must deliberately move from the private to the public sphere and confront the different structures, systems, policies and issues

1 *Brian Friel: Plays1* (London: Faber and Faber: 1996 *Translations* pp. 377–451), p. 445.

which continue to keep women bound. Systematic social analysis will heighten awareness about the social context of our lives and will blatantly demonstrate the need for radical social change.

Social Analysis and the Imagination

I will propose that social analysis, in the manner required, is imaginative work both at the level of diagnosis and of treatment. To stand back from the familiar and the given, to be able to unravel present reality in order to name its history, its meaning, its original arrangement, is an imaginative act. The imaginative deconstruction of present structures and systems, such as language, unleashes a requisite freedom because it shifts the image of permanency which surrounds male dominance and allows us to see it as an historical pattern simply riding the river of time.

Empowering people to think structurally is also imaginative work. Many people can quietly name the oppression of their own individual lives but they find it extremely difficult to see the roots of oppression entangled around the structures of the society which they uncritically support. Paolo Freire, the great Brazilian educator, found that in the four-step process towards raising critical consciousness it was the poets, the artists and the songwriters who had the greatest capacity to move through what he calls the 'splitting of consciousness' to the awakening to social oppression.[2] Those who have the capacity to interpret reality imaginatively have a more fluid relationship with 'fixed' structures, are able to name their oppressiveness and can often spark similar insight in others, which otherwise would remain dormant.

2 Paolo Freire, *Pedagogy of the Oppressed* (New York: The Seabury Press, 1970).

Language: The Cornerstone of Monoreality

The oppression of women at a structural level is a multifaceted phenomenon. I contend, however, that the cornerstone which keeps the edifice of male dominance and monoreality in place is language. I agree with Chris Weedon when she argues:

> The meaning of the existing structures of social institutions, as much as the structures themselves and the subject positions which they offer their subjects, is a site of political struggle waged mainly though not exclusively in language.[3]

Language is an integral part of patriarchy; it is never neutral. It is the mortar which holds structures together and maintains male power. Luce Irigaray reminds us that 'the dwelling which seems to form the essence of his maleness is language'.[4] The symbolic order is a male construction. The discourse that dominates our lives represents a male imagination. To engage in social analysis, motivated by a passion to transform the systemic oppression of women, would be impossible without a radical discourse analysis: a critique of the language which envelops our lives. For language is the site where the social individual is constructed, it is the context where culture and consciousness meet, it is the place where gender and power are. Therefore, we ignore it at our peril. Yet to tinker with words is dangerous work. Audre Lorde's poem 'Thaw' reminds us that this work is as precarious as stepping on melting ice.[5]

The pervasive infiltration of language through the very pores of our being and knowing, makes the critique of discourse a complex and multifarious task. This is evidenced by the multiple theories that different feminist linguists offer us on language. In order to posit an understanding of language that recognises sexual difference and allows men and women to

3 Chris Weedon, *Feminist Practice and Poststructuralist Theory* (London: Basil Blackwell, 1987), pp. 37–38.

4 Luce Irigaray, *An Ethics of Sexual Difference*, p. 127.

5 *Thaw* from *The Marvellous Arithmetics of Distance Poems 1987–1992* (New York: W.W. Norton & Company, 1993), p. 10.

engage in discourses of mutual exchange, I will first offer an overview of four of these theories.

Feminist Linguistics

Man-Made Words

Among feminist linguists Dale Spender's work has received the most popular acclaim.

As the title of her well-known book Man Made Language indicates, she believes that meaning is literally man-made.[6] At birth women are plunged into a pre-existent sea of male symbols and spend their lives swimming against the tide of this alien current.

Women are constantly exiled from giving meaning to their experience as women because all that is available to them is man-made language: 'Women who wish to express themselves must translate their experience into the male code.'[7] This presents women with a double bind because it denies, discounts and defines women and women's experiences.[8] Thus women feel either muted or tongue-tied and simply lapse into silence or else they try to express themselves in an 'alien language'. Spender explains: 'Women are muted because men are in control of the language, and the meanings and the knowledge of women cannot be accounted for outside of that male control.'[9] A simple example of this male control of language is the fact that men continue to assume legal rights to name their spouses after themselves. This custom assumes that genealogical authority belongs to men alone. A non-stratified society would share that authority

6 Dale Spender, *Man Made Language* (London: Routledge & Kegan Paul, 1980).

7 Ibid., p. 81.

8 C. Kramarae, *Women and Men Speaking: Frameworks for Analysis* (Rowley, MA: Newbury House Publishers, 1981).

9 *Ibid*, p. 83 and p. 77.

between women and men. The power to name is closely connected with the right to control. The permission given to 'man' in the book of Genesis to name and master nature has translated into a cultural right to tame and domesticate women.[10]

Rendering women incapable of expressing their experience in meaningful language is one of the constraints of man-made language; giving men inordinate control over women's lives is yet another. However, Spender's analysis does not end here. She also highlights the link between perception and language, stating that the language used to describe reality shapes our perception of that reality. From their first receptive moments girl children hear reality shaped by patriarchal terminology.

> Language … is not merely a vehicle which carries ideas. It is itself a shaper of ideas … what we see in the world around us depends in a large part on the principles we have encoded in language.[11]

Dale Spender's position could be described as linguistic determinism. She believes that language is the root cause of women's oppression. Her critique is radical and single- minded. It is language that teaches women that they are inferior and it is language that maintains structures of male power. It is language that tells women and girl children that they should be seen and not heard. In 1989 Dale Spender taped sixteen different conversations that took place between academic women and an assortment of academic men. She concealed the tape recorder and later requested they listen to the tapes to analyse patterns of conversations to which all agreed. Before commencing her analysis, she asked one question: 'Do you think you had a fair share of the conversation?' All the women said yes, one declaring that she had more than her share; twelve men said yes, and four said no. The following is an account of her findings: 'When I had analysed these tapes I found that fourteen feminists who believed that they had a fair share of the conversation spoke between 8 per cent and 38 per cent of the time. In this group were two of the men who were of the opinion that they had not had a fair share and they spoke for 75 per

10 A similar point is made by Kramarae, 1981, p. 26.

11 Dale Spender, *Man Made Language* p. 139.

cent and 67 per cent of the time respectively.'[12] Wittgenstein's axiom 'the master of the language is the master of us all' which is rooted in the assumption that 'it is the world of words that creates the world of things' is a viewpoint that Spender, albeit for different reasons, would accept.[13]

Public vs. Private Words

The single-mindedness of Dale Spender's critique has certain advantages. It highlights language as central in shaping meaning and maintaining a social order of male dominance. Yet the deterministic tendencies of this viewpoint leaves some with an image of women as helpless victims, consigned to a world of silence. As I indicated in Chapter One, this belies the truth of women's lives. Other readers of Spender can feel burdened with the impossible task of having to create a totally new language to express women's experiences. The enormity of this challenge can bring a new sense of paralysis and ultimately add to the feeling of being 'an outsider', a feeling Spender sets out to critique.[14]

Deborah Cameron and Cora Kaplan offer a more nuanced treatment of the oppressiveness of language when they call for a distinction between private and public uses of language. While women can communicate most effectively in the private sphere, 'they are institutionally constrained and

12 Dale Spender, *The Writing or the Sex* (New York: Pergamon Press, 1989) pp. 9–10.

13 As quoted by Jacques Lacan in *The Language of the Self: The Function of Language in Psychoanalysis*, trans. Anthony Wilden (Baltimore: John Hopkins University Press, 1968), p. 39. Lacan's own viewpoint that 'women are constructed in the domain of the male sign and therefore they are excluded by the nature of things' would also find parallels in Spender's critique.

14 An excellent critique of Dale Spender's position can be found in an article by Carolyn Stone, '"Blocking Women's Meanings": Philosophical Critique of Spender's Account of the Maleness of English in Man Made Language.' in *New Writing by Women in Philosophy*, ed. by Mowenna Griffiths and Margaret Whitford (University of Nottingham, 1996) pp. 174–185.

negatively judged in the public (male) arena'.[15] In fact women among women often experience a depth of sharing and a level of communication unknown in mixed or all-male company. Women are denied access to the most influential and prestigious registers of language. Men control the 'high' language of public discourse and this 'refusal of access to public language is one of the major forms of the oppression of women within a social class as well as intraclass situations'.[16]

This critique of the male control of public language is found within the sociolinguistic school and is less absolute in its claims. While authors such as Cameron and Kaplan would agree that language oppresses women they would insist that it is not the sole agent of women's oppression. For example, the prelinguistic child is shaped and formed by the image of patriarchy far sooner than sexism is put into words. The girl child dressed in pink and surrounded by the frills of femininity imbibes a socialisation that is sexist far sooner than she can conceptually reflect on the heritage that is hers. As she develops, the images of infancy will spin and shape into social and political words which will continue to restrict her.

While sociolinguistics situates a critique of language within a social context, this does not render that critique any less radical; rather it grounds it in the real and allows us recognise ways we can act to effect social change. The challenge for women is to name their experiences and articulate their understanding of reality in ways that shape public policy. Where social practice permits men to interrupt, to mediate or to speak for women, women must simply assume responsibility for their own voice and speak through the barriers that have excluded them in the past. Attention to language practices can be a crucial way of unmasking 'the politics of everyday life'.[17] A first step towards 'desilencing' women can take place within the context of feminist group work. Here women can 'hear each other into speech', breaking the silence of their lives, learning to whisper secrets that have been

15 Deborah Cameron, *Feminism – Linguistic Theory* (London: Macmillan, 1990), p. 168.

16 Cora Kaplan, 'Language and Gender', *Papers on Patriarchy* (Women's Publishing Collective, 1976), p. 21.

17 Mary Crawford, Talking Difference: *On Gender and Language* (London: Sage Publications 1995) p. 180.

locked within the private sphere. As women learn from one another, they come to know how to develop strategies that will impact the public world.

The problem with our present language is the way it has shaped women as social beings, as persons living and acting in society. It has dictated how girl children and women should behave in public life. If the silencing of educated women still persists in the public rituals of our society one can only imagine how the uneducated, the poor or the racially oppressed fare in this regard. As Alice Walker questions:

> How was the creativity of the black woman kept alive, year after year and century after century, when for most of the years black people have been in America, it was a punishable crime for a black person to read and write?[18]

It is indeed a cause for wonderment, an example of the resilience of the human spirit, that races and peoples who have been so oppressed have managed, especially through the oral word, to keep their traditions alive. The writer bell hooks, an African American, who grew up in a Southern black community, recalls from her experience how difficult it was to sustain speech amidst racial oppression:

> I was never taught absolute silence, I was taught that it was important to speak but to talk a talk that was itself a silence. Taught to speak and beware of the betrayal of too much speech, I experienced intense confusion and deep anxiety in my efforts to speak and write. [19]

Brian Friel's play *Translations* is also about this struggle, albeit in a different land. [20] As Friel himself describes it, it is 'a play about the death of the Irish language and the acquisition of English and the profound effects that that change-over would have on a people'.[21] Set in the small Irish-speaking Donegal community of Baile Beag/Ballybeg in 1833, the

18 Alice Walker, *In Search of Our Mother's Gardens* (London: Women's Press, 1984), p. 234.

19 bell hooks. *Talking Back: Thinking Feminist, Thinking Black* (Boston: South End Press 1989), p. 7.

20 Brian Friel's play *Translations* was first staged by the Field Day Theatre Company in the Guildhall, Derry in 23 September 1980.

21 Brian Friel, *The Crane Bag*, Vol. 7 No. 2, p. 122.

play explores the effects of the Ordnance Survey of Ireland as local place-names are changed from Irish to English. The play also analyses the attempts by the English to close down the local hedge school which is held in a disused barn and to open an English-speaking National school. Friel comments: 'Because their townland is being renamed everything that was familiar is becoming strange.' The lack of respect for the language difference of the local people is evidenced by the comments of the translator Owen: 'My job is to translate the quaint, archaic tongue that you people persist in speaking into the King's good English.'[22]

Language is a powerful political tool and in the hands of the colonisers has been used to render the familiar strange. The deliberate removal of their language erodes the very identity of a people, something the powerful have always known and acted on.

'It's an eviction of sorts.'[23]

The school teacher Hugh summarises the aftermath of being left in a 'translated' condition: 'It can happen that a civilisation can be imprisoned in a linguistic contour which no longer matches the landscape of … fact.'[24] The eviction from a common language can cause a disorientation that leaves a profound mark on the psyche. Irish poet John Montague traces the trauma of this experience in his poem 'A Grafted Tongue':

> (Dumb,
> Bloodied, the severed
> head now chokes to
> speak another tongue—
> ....
> To grow
> a second tongue, as

22 Brian Friel, *Translations* (London: Faber and Faber, 1981), p. 404.

23 Brian Friel, *Translations*, p. 420.

24 Brian Friel, *Translations*, p. 419. Friel's treatment of language in this play. *Translations*, is more highly nuanced than these brief comments may suggest. While the play bemoans the imposed loss of a people's native tongue it also cautions against language fossilisation and calls for the constant renewal and growth of language. I am indebted to Dr Patrick Burke, St Patrick's College Drumcondra, Dublin Ireland whose work on Brian Friel has inspired these comments.

harsh a humiliation,
as twice to be bom.[25]

This critique of the colonial, racist pattern of erasing the original language of the oppressed group is not intended as a romanticisation of the mother-tongue (read father-tongue). As we become inhabitants of a global village, we all recognise that we live between translations. To remain doggedly monolingual is ultimately to lose one's voice. Rather it is an attempt to heighten awareness, to raise consciousness about the links between language and identity at both an individual and a socio-cultural level.

People's 'eviction' from their full potential is also achieved by keeping vast numbers of the world population illiterate. It comes as a surprise to some to realise that 950 million people remain illiterate in this world of ours. One in three women is illiterate as opposed to one in every five men. In developing countries, 45 per cent of women are illiterate.[26] The reasons for this situation are not simply economic but are also political. Removing the possibility for these people to enter the public discourse by keeping them illiterate allows the powerful to rule with little fear of critique or opposition. This point was concretised in the life of Paulo Freire, a Brazilian born in 1921. Aware of how many of his people were 'living corpses', victimised by lack of education, he developed an extraordinarily successful literacy programme which spread rapidly throughout north-eastern Brazil. The response of his government was firstly to imprison him and later to deport him.[27]

A sociolinguistic perspective raises women's consciousness to the realisation that the self cannot be separated from the social structure of which it is a part and that the mortar which will hold the bricks of a new society

25 John Montague, 'A Grafted Tongue', *New Selected Poems* (Oldcastle: Gallery Press, 1989), pp. 49–50.

26 These statistics are provided by John Micklos, Jr. in his article: 'Women and World Literacy', in Education Digest December 1996, pp. 41–45.

27 Friere's books *Pedagogy of the Oppressed and Pedagogy of IIope* (Stew York: The Continuum Publishing Company, 1992), chronicle this work.

together must be an inclusive language articulated publicly from both female and male experience.

Words in Flux

A third set of linguistics would fall within the poststructuralist and postmodernist schools. Theorists within these groupings would agree that language is not some ethereal system; rather it is rooted in the social and historical soil of life. Their primary area of concern is to shift our perception of language and the social structures which envelop us as fixed realities, to a view that reality, ourselves, and of course language are in a state of flux, of movement. We don't live in a fixed order of reality; rather a radical transitoriness marks all of existence.

Feminist poststructuralists and postmodernists also encourage us to name the plurality within which we live. As stated earlier, there is not just one language, one type of public discourse, one way of being human. In fact, if we open our eyes and bring into focus the richness that surrounds us, we could shift our acceptance of the dominant way of being as the only way of being. It is within this context that liberal humanism is critiqued as the one path to human transformation. As Zillah Eisenstein argues correctly,

> though feminism emerged from the theories and practices of liberalism concerning individual autonomy, it has to undermine liberalism's foundation both in terms of the hidden principles of autonomy and individuality and in terms of the institutionalisation of the separation between the public and private realms.[28]

Liberalism's concern for the well-being of the individual is a noble aspiration which no one would contest. However, as long as our social systems and structures favour the full humanity of some over that of others we must place our energies with oppressed groups in the political and social struggle against racial and class injustice. Feminists also question

28 Zillah Eisenstein, *The Radical Future of Liberal Feminism* (Boston: Northeastern University Press, 1981).

the 'gender-blindness' of liberalism. Cameron astutely comments: 'While it is possible to admit women to "mankind" and to extend to them the restricted rights of liberalism, it is another thing to challenge humanist conceptions of "man", woman and the nature of language.'[29] My main critique of liberal humanism is of its arrogance and its pretence that the liberal vision offers the final solution to the human quest for meaning. Feminist poststructuralism shakes the foundations of the familiar and asks us to recognise the multiple, yet often hidden, discourses that are in fact shaping who we are and/or hindering who we wish to become. Language is a central agent in shaping our understanding of ourselves and society's self-understanding. Cameron notes:

> For poststructuralist theory the common factor in the analysis of social organisation, social meanings, power and individual consciousness, is language. Language is the place where actual and possible forms of social organisation and their likely social and political consequence are defined and contested. Yet it is also the place where our sense of ourselves, our subjectivity, is constructed.[30]

A feminist poststructuralist position lifts women from the mire of monoreality and oppression by allowing them to recognise that the way things are is not the way they have to be. There is no god-given natural law sanctifying the present situation as if it always was and always will be. In fact, our subjectivity is fashioned in the social environment in which we live by the language users who surround our lives. We live amidst many discourses be they political, economic, social. By communicating in richly diverse contexts, by respecting differences and coaxing otherness, new words will emerge, new ways of being will be envisaged.

It was Freud who originally called in question the concept of a human being as fixed and unified, a completed entity. His work made possible a radically altered understanding of what a human being is, namely, a work in progress. Feminist poststructuralism brings these insights to the lives of women and challenges women to bring to consciousness the hidden

29 Cameron, op. cit, p. 168.

30 Ibid, p. 21.

meanings that shape their oppression. The challenge is to recognise the different discourses that name male dominance as natural and then to act freely in order to create a radically new discourse. Suddenly the sacrosanct realms of objectivity and universality are unveiled for what they are; sanctuaries preserving male power.

Sexually Different Words

The final strand of linguistic theory which I would like to examine lies within the work of French feminist philosopher Luce Irigaray.

In my treatment of Irigaray's position in Chapter One, I demonstrated her critique of male normativity as the preoccupation with 'sameness'. In her writings she shows that it is above all language that maintains this sameness.

> If we keep on speaking the same language together, we're going to reproduce the same history … If we keep on speaking sameness, if we speak to each other as men have been doing for centuries, as we have been taught to speak, we'll miss each other, fail ourselves.[31]

This failure of patriarchy to accept difference, this need to reduce everything to phallic oneness has led to a subsuming of women and women's lives within male discourse. Irigaray alerts us to 'the movement to speak of the "other" in a language systematised by/for the same'.[32] The challenge is 'to come out of their language' and to create a language which would reflect the identity of both female and male lives. This must be rooted in a new recognition and acceptance of sexual difference. If, as I have stated, women have been excluded from symbolic representation in the system of sameness, then 'it must be women themselves who must take

31 Luce Irigaray, *This Sex Which Is Not One*, p. 205.

32 Luce Irigaray, *Speculum of the Other Woman*, trans. Gillian G. Gill (Ithaca: Cornell University Press, 1985), p. 139.

part in releasing the real from its point of systemic closure, to create a new symbolic'.[33] Such breaking open of the potential of language to represent sexual difference will allow us to move beyond the monologic, the homogeneity of words that we have inherited.

If women find their own subjectivity and articulate publicly the truthful discourse of their lives, then men could relax and return within themselves and simply feel an obligation to speak from the inside of their own experiences rather than to stand 'outside' experience. We then would 'return the masculine to its own language, leaving open the possibility of a different language. That means that the masculine would no longer be "everything" '.[34] I have little doubt that new social relationships, relationships of mutual respect and love, would emerge if men and women began talking from a perspective that takes sexual difference seriously.

Irigaray posits that for the work of sexual difference to take place we need 'a revolution in thought and ethics'.[35] The transformation of language in the manner in which she proposes is a matter of social justice. Indeed, social injustice against women will never be eradicated until we change our language.

> Social justice and especially sexual justice cannot be achieved without changing the laws of language and the conceptions of truths and values structuring the social order.[36]

It is clear that the radical reform of a social system that continues to suppress women is dependent on a linguistic revolution. For example, the injustice of violent crimes against women is augmented by the silence which encases them. We must engage in 'disruptive tactics' in order to crack open the present codes of communication. If, as is evident, the present social order is built on the silence, the passivity and the repression of women's voices, then women-made languages, articulated from a

33 Caroline Williams, 'Feminism, Subjectivity and Psychoanalysis,' in *Knowing the Difference*, eds, Kathleen Lennon and Margaret Whitford (London: Routledge 1994), p. 175.

34 Luce Irigaray, *This Sex Which Is Not One*, p. 80.

35 Irigaray, 'Sexual Difference,' in Toril Moi, ed. *French Feminist Thought: A Reader* (London: Basil Blackwell, 1988), p. 119.

36 Irigaray, *Je, tu, Nous*, p. 22.

perspective of sexual difference, would shake the foundation of the social order. And, 'if we made the foundation of the social order shift, then everything will shift'.[37]

Such 'disruptive tactics', such shaking of the foundations of the present social system, requires that we make visible the links between sexuality and language. Working from a philosophical and psychoanalytic base, Irigaray critiques Freud's failure to distinguish the female and male libidos. Freud, 'enmeshed in a structure and an ideology of the patriarchal type' writes as if, 'there is but one sexual drive, that of the male'.[38] Female sexuality, female desire, is not, as male psychoanalysts claim, a hankering after maleness (penis envy and phallic fantasy). Female desire is unique and distinct, has its own 'specificity', but has not come to expression in male discourse, which is, to date, the only public discourse available. Women must enflesh their words fearlessly into speech, into public speech.

An awareness of sexual difference challenges women to give symbolic representation to our bodies. If we are to claim our identity as sexual subjects, then we must speak our corporeality, our sensuality, into the public discourse. As Julia Kristeva recommends 'break the code … shatter language … find a specific discourse closer to the body and emotions, to the unnameable repressed by the social contract'.[39] In calling women to write their bodies into speech, Irigaray is exposing the single sexed nature of the present phallocratic discourse. It is vital that we see the connection between sexuality and language and then open up language to represent sexual difference.

> If we don't invent a language, if we don't find our body's language, it will have too few gestures to accompany our story. We shall tire of the same ones, and leave our desires unexpressed, unrealised. Asleep again, unsatisfied, we shall fall back upon the words of men – who for their part, have 'known' for a long time. But not our body.[40]

37 Irigaray, 'Women-Mothers, the Silent Substratum of the Social Order', trans. David Macey in *The Irigaray Reader*, ed. Margaret Whitford (Oxford: Blackwell, 1991), p. 47.

38 Irigaray, *This Sex Which Is Not One*, p. 70.

39 Kristeva, 'Women's Time', in *The Kristeva Reader,* ed. T. Moi (Oxford: Basil Blackwell, 1986),p. 200.

40 Luce Irigaray, *This Sex Which Is Not One*, p. 214.

If the phallic symbol determines the oneness, the fixity, the single-minded trajectory of male discourse, Irigaray suggests that the metaphor of the 'two lips' could open the imagination to the possibilities of female language. It would be a discourse marked by fluidity and plurality:

> Between our lips, yours and mine, several voices, several ways of speaking resound endlessly, back and forth. One is never separable from the other. I/you: we are always several at once. And how could one dominate the other? Impose her voice, her tone, her meaning?[41]

It is vital to understand that Irigaray is not seeking in her writing to create a new dichotomy between 'the phallus' and 'the lips', rather she is attempting to refigure sexual difference by evoking the metaphor of her 'sex' as a difference that overflows any rigid logic of definition.[42] Her desire is to break the hegemony of the phallocratic narrative and to call men and women to a different way of being together. If we are to cross the threshold to this new future, women must speak through their bodies and men and women must recognise the link between sexuality and language.

To journey forward, we must go back through 'the masculine imagery, to interpret the way it has reduced us to silence, to muteness or mimicry, and I am attempting, from that starting point and at the same time, to (re)discover a possible space for feminine imagery'.[43] Male cultural imagery hangs in the air all around us and infiltrates every breath we breathe. The patriarchal symbolic system is born of a male imagination and the omnipresence of such imagery has duped people into equating the symbolic with the real. Irigaray challenges the all-pervasive nature of this male 'imaginaire' and queries its claims to express absolute truth. The way forward is to discover a space for the female imagination to come to public expression in language.[44]

41 Ibid, p. 209.

42 Drucilla Cornell, *Beyond Accommodation*, p. 19.

43 Irigaray, *This Sex Which Is Not One*, p. 164.

44 Margaret Whitford reminds us that in the development of her writing Irigaray wrests the concept of the imaginary from its colonised treatment by Lacan and gradually 'the imaginary emerges from its relatively subordinate position in Speculum to become in, *The Sex*, and *Ethique*, one of the key notions of an

Women's imaginative language will be pluriform in expression because women's capacity for sexual pleasure is pluriform. It would be rhythmic and spiralling, not linear and fixed. To allow women's bodiliness to shape public discourse could indeed herald the advent of a new imaginative poetics, a new syntax. Irigaray remarks:

> First of all I would say it has nothing to do with the syntax which we have used for centuries, namely, that constructed according to the following organisation: subject, predicate, or subject, verb, object. For female sexuality is not unifiable, it cannot be subsumed under the concept of subject which brings into question all the syntactical norms.[45]

Luce Irigaray is challenging women to formulate a new syntax, a construction of language that will revalue the female and express what it is to be female and sexually different in public discourse. As I have indicated, the struggle is social and structural and radically political. There is no precedence for the task ahead, no blueprint to dictate the way forward. The patriarchal language system which surrounds us is all-pervasive. However, the task is clear: if women are to claim their identity, their own subjectivity as women, then they must shape the symbolic system with images and words that emanate from the specificity of female existence.

Towards the end of this chapter I will broach the question: how can this be done? How can we creatively and imaginatively construct a discourse that reflects sexual difference and promotes mutual relationship? But first it is important, in light of this fourfold critique and challenge from the different schools of feminist linguistics, to examine further how women have been bound by words. As a theologian and educator, I have a specific interest in raising critical awareness about the role that religious language has played and continues to play in promoting male monologic and in rendering women silent, mute or passively accepting of a system that oppresses them.

---

ambitious social critique.' See Whitford, *Luce Irigaray: Philosophy in the Feminine* (London: Routledge, 1991), p. 66.

45 Luce Irigaray, 'Women's Exile: Interview with Luce Irigaray,' *Ideology and Consciousness*, 1, p. 64.

Language of the Male Religious Imagination

The all-pervasive 'man-made language', which Spender cautions against, is integral to the inheritance of church teaching within official church documents. Furthermore, the anthropology underpinning these teachings is profoundly dualistic because it promotes the notion of difference as that which is 'less than'. Over the centuries, the church has been one of the most influential reinforcers of oppressive gender patterns. According to its teachings, women by nature represent carnality, change and temporality. Her natural biological sexual drives must be controlled and channelled towards their reproductive end. All social mores and constraints on women are in place to contain and control her lesser, sinful condition.

Woman as 'Subservient to Man'

As far back as the fourth century, St Augustine cautioned women that any break from their passive submissive role of obedience to men – who hold rationality and truth – is to risk the sin of pride. Augustine believed that Eve would not have been open to temptation 'if there was not already within her heart a love of her own independence and a proud presumption on self which through that temptation was destined to be found out and cast down'.[46] Indeed, Augustine spoke of pride, using female metaphors: 'Pride carries a daughter, envy, in her train.'[47] So the assertive, self-determined woman is heading for perdition.

This tradition of cautioning women against pride and promoting an image of women as passive and subservient to men, has continued into our own century. In 1930, Pius XI in his encyclical Casti Connubii counselled women that any aspirations towards equality were debasing and unnatural. Pius XII extended the Pauline tradition by exhorting women to be

46 *De Genesi adLitteram* 11.30.39 PL. 34.445.

47 *De Sante Virginitate* 30 PL 46 412 NPNF, Series 1 Volume 3.

submissive to their husbands: 'Many voices will suggest rather a proud autonomy; they will repeat that you are in every respect the equal to your husband, and in many respects his superior. Do not react like Eve to these lying, tempting deceitful voices.'[48]

Some may feel that we have long outgrown the outlandish council that such teachings impart. However, working with women, especially in disadvantaged areas, and watching them struggle with issues of confidence and self-empowerment and autonomy, I am convinced that the residue of these dictates still seeps down through the generations and continues to haunt women, if not consciously then unconsciously. Elizabeth Cady Stanton's quip in the nineteenth century that 'self-realisation is a higher duty for women than self-sacrifice' remains as true today, one century later. I have watched women who claim their own power, their own pride, and who step outside the self-sacrificing roles of wife and mother in order to become leaders in their local community, suffer the charge of being 'uppity', of 'having notions beyond their station'. Such jeering is but the external manifestation of a residual 'orthodox' imagery and language that programmes women to be meek and submissive, seen but not heard. The 'good' woman knows her place on the echelons of the divinely ordained hierarchy.

Woman as 'Feminine and Masculine'

Classical theology is riddled with linguistic formulations which fossilise the oppression of women. Further examples from Augustine illustrate how his anthropology is rooted in a dualistic paradigm and necessitates a hierarchical structure which is held in place by the oppression of women. Men and women are made up of bodies and spirits. Gender distinctions

48 Pius XI, *Casti Connubii*, 1930, in *The Woman in the Modern World: Papal Teachings*, eds, Benedictine Monks of Solesines (Boston: St Paul Editions, 1959), pp. 37–38 and in the same collection Pius XII, 'To all Newlyweds,' September 1941, pp. 68–69.

relate only to the bodies of men and women. However, in the mind, the higher reality, there exists a further dualism. Augustine distinguishes between the masculine and the feminine functions of the mind. He names the masculine function as higher than the feminine and his conclusion that only the masculine aspect of the mind can image God follows with impeccable logic.[49]

Women possess the image of God in the masculine dimension of her rational soul, but in the bodily incarnation of the soul she is *femina* and thus represents the inferior aspects of the soul and is inferior to man. Woman therefore in the masculine aspects of her mind can image God (a way of conceding to Genesis 121). However, in her body she symbolises the feminine or lesser function of the mind and therefore cannot image God (a way of concurring with 1 Corinthians 11:7). To quote Augustine:

> How then did the Apostle tell us that the man is the image of God, and therefore he is forbidden to cover his head, but that the woman is not so and therefore is commanded to cover hers? Unless for sooth, according to that which I have said already, when I was treating of the human mind, that the woman together with her own husband is the image of God, so that whole substance may be one image, but when she is referred separately to her quality of help-mate, which regards the woman herself alone, then she is not the image of God, but as regards the man alone, he is the image of God as fully and completely as when the woman is joined with him in one.[50]

This passage is a superb example of the logical precision of 'man-made language', a logic which is rooted in the normativity of male superiority. There is *no* understanding of the social context of language; rather women's inferiority is God-given and preordained in the nature of things. Reality is fixed and static and language simply reflects the facts. Although Augustine employs the concept of masculine and feminine to reflect dimensions of the human psyche which are to be distinguished from corporeal man and woman, the absence of gender difference in the masculine and feminine does not free these concepts from being oppressive. While a woman may have a masculine and a feminine dimension to her mind, the 'feminine only images God when it is united to the masculine, which

49 *De Trinitate*, PL 42.12.13.21.

50 Ibid, 12.7.10.

always reflects God's image.'[51] So 'the feminine', whether in the male or female psyche, reflects the inferior qualities of womanhood.

Woman as 'Different but Equal'

The memory of this linguistic past influences the present and continues to penetrate church documents even to our day. Take the letter *Mulieris Dignitatem* from Pope John Paul II (15 August 1988). This document pays lip service to the principles of equality; at last women are not spoken of as ontologically inferior. However, the concretisation of these principles is blocked by an anthropology of complementarity that is still reflective of the writings of Augustine. Men and women continue to be viewed through a dualistic lens. In a recent interview, the Catholic Archbishop of Dublin, Desmond Connell, was questioned about the possibility of women becoming equal partners in the power structures of the Church. His response was telling: 'Well now, the whole problem of equality is an extraordinarily difficult problem. Equality sounds very good as a slogan but there is such a thing also as difference between people and each making their own proper contribution and this in its own way is a form of equality. If you take the family, the wife cannot be the husband and the husband cannot be the wife; that doesn't mean they're not equal.'[52] Men and women are different but equal, we are told. However, if 'difference' is defined within a hierarchical framework then mutuality is impossible. The *anthropology of complementarity* (which pervades the document) divides men and women into two opposite ways of being and consequently blocks any of the new aspirations for a Church beyond sexism becoming a reality.

51 I have been assisted in these reflections by the work of Kim E. Power, *Augustine's Theology of Women: Influences and Implications*, Thesis presented to Melbourne University, p. 96.

52 This interview was part of the R.T.E. television programme *Would You Believe*. Feb. 23, 1997.

In the Pope's letter *Mulieris Dignitatem*, the terms 'masculinity' and 'femininity' are employed throughout, once again revealing the divisiveness of this terminology. The letter argues that women must not become masculine:

> Even the rightful opposition of women to what is expressed in biblical words 'He shall rule over you' (Gen 3:16) must not under any condition lead to the 'masculinisation' of women. In the name of liberation from male 'domination', women must not appropriate to themselves male characteristics contrary to their own feminine originality.

On the other hand, the male is exhorted to develop his femininity. In the symbolic spousal relationship between God and his people, 'the symbol of Bridegroom is masculine' and men are included in the concept of the Bride (p. 25). The feminine as inferior is of course accessible to the male. However, the masculine as superior, indeed divinely related, is accessible to men only.

Such language is not as benign as it may appear. As long as such outmoded anthropology is linguistically sustained, the image of woman as 'lesser than', as 'other' than 'the same' is being projected and promoted. The following outbursts of fear and hatred of women by Augustine would not be fashionable today but the undercurrent of such imagery persists in the most recent church documents:

> You may paint her in the most flattering colours and endow her with every gift, but there is nothing I am more determined to avoid than relations with a woman. I feel that there is nothing which so degrades the high intelligence of a man than the embraces of a woman and the contact with her body, without which it is impossible to possess a wife.[53]

There is a blatant honesty and a deep consistency in the writings of church fathers such as Augustine – their anthropology leads them to the conclusion that women are the weaker sex. For example, Augustine frequently

53 Augustine, Soliloq. 1, 10.17 PL.33. Col. 878. Kari Borreson, *Subordination and Equivalence: The Nature and Role of Woman in Augustine and Thomas Aquinas* (Washington, DC: University Press of America, 1981).

speaks of woman as 'muliercula' (mere woman) and never hides his belief that women are subordinate to men.

There is less consistency – and less honesty – in the teachings of the contemporary fathers. In recent documents on women from the official church sources, the dualistic anthropology remains in place but the language used is deceptive and seeks to cloak reality. To tell women that they are equal to men and then to illustrate this equality by using dualistic language of femininity and masculinity with its underlying premise that masculinity is superior, is simply to engage in 'double-speak'. Such language rings in the ears of conscientised women as utterly meaningless and untrue.

The political discourse used by the men of the church to exclude women from priesthood is a perfect example of such rhetoric. To tell women that they are equal to men in principle but to block their concrete participation as full members in the ministries of their church is an example of man-made language seeking to preserve the bastion of man-made power. For their words to have any credibility they must be given institutional recognition.

One of the more honest explanations for the exclusion of women from the priesthood was articulated in 1962 by Emmanuel D'Lorenzo, OMI in his work on the sacrament of orders. At the time D'Lorenzo was Professor of Theology at the Catholic University of America, Washington, DC. He firmly believed that

> the reason … for denying women the right to teach is a reason that is absolute and universal, based as it is on the natural condition of inferiority and subjection that is the portion of women … This moral feebleness is manifest at once in lightness of judgement, in credulity … and finally in the fragility of spirit by which she is less able to rein in the passions, particularly concupiscence. [54]

A similar perspective albeit using a different medium was voiced recently by the character of Tommy in Michael Harding's brilliant play *Misogynist*. Tommy, a man in his fifties and a religious fanatic, adopts the persona of a priest engulfed in the extremes of clericalism. In his attic turned belfry,

54 Emmanuel D'Lorenzo, *Sacrament of Orders* as quoted in 'Does the Church Discriminate Against Women on the Basis of Their Sex?' by Catherine Beaton, Critic June–July 1966, pp. 21–27.

he gives vent to his worst fears in misogynist monologues. The old order is crumbling, he muses, 'the creeping rot, disintegration, the degeneration of history'.[55] The greatest threat in this post-modern time is the threat posed by women. It is their presence, their arrogant assumption that they too could lift the chalice and say the holy words that could finally push us over the precipice to chaos.

> Her frivolous hands dare to trespass on the alter that and seeketh out the Holy Chalice.[56]

Tommy, in conversation with his alter-ego on video, concludes that this threat must be squashed.

A young woman in starched shortie surplus punctuates his sayings by her presence. At times he condemns her as the temptress personified and calls on his brothers to beware:

> My brothers we have fought many battles many adversaries over the years. But this little lizard in the grass is the worst of them all. In the sweet fragrance of the grass, with her kind words, gently cloaking the fangs of poison. This is the most deadly enemy of all Yes?[57]

At other times her presence moves him to violence and he verbally abuses her, shouting: 'Leave her blood on the wall.'[58] At another point in the play, he physically threatens her with a knife.

The play is an excellent dramatic expression of the seething anger and fear which erupts when the exclusive club of clericalism is challenged. The encroachment of feminism on the all-male preserve of religious tradition uncovers all that is negative in a tradition that excludes one half of the human race from full participation. Indeed it is the challenge of feminism

55 *Misogynist* by Michael Harding from *The Crack in the Emerald: New Irish Plays I:* (London: Faber and Faber, 1996), p. 158. (All citations were originally from an unpublished manuscript of Misogynist, that was supplied by the Irish author, Michael Harding, in personal correspondence. Ann Louise saw it performed in the Abbey, 1990 and wrote to the author after that).

56 *Misogynist*, p. 179.

57 *Misogynist*, p. 167.

58 *Misogynist, p.* 167.

with its aspiration for mutuality between men and women that unveils an exclusivist male tradition for what it is: misogynist.

Sociolinguists such as Cameron and Kaplan have shown in their analysis that women have been blocked from shaping the public discourse of both State and Church. Ordaining women would give women access to public language which their present exclusion prohibits. Today in the Catholic Church women are not only blocked from performing the public rituals of their church, the new Code of Canon Law even prohibits them preaching a homily. Thus the public discourse of the Roman Catholic Church is entirely controlled by men. Excluding women from centres of power in church communities, preventing them from shaping public ideas and taking official decisions, not only stifles their potential but also ensures that the full truth of human experience cannot come to expression. To interpret divine meaning simply from male experience is to miss the harmony of insight possible when mutuality is given voice.

Another form of excluding women from shaping the public discourse of Christian communities is the persistent use of sexist language both in church documents and church speech. Calls by feminists for inclusive language have met with varying degrees of resistance. This, according to linguists Miller and Swift, should not surprise us: 'At a deep level changes in a language are threatening because they signal widespread changes in social mores.'[59] Indeed, some people express great openness to the vision and goal of feminism but when it means interfering with language they withdraw their support. A typical example of such inconsistency is offered by Stephen Kaufer: 'The feminist attack on social crimes may be as legitimate as it was inevitable. But the attack on words is only another social crime – one against the means and hope of communication.'[60]

Such a statement expresses the deep intuition that the male monopoly on power and discourse will alter if the keystone of sexist language is removed. There is also a fear that if we move the fixed pillar of male language, stable society will disintegrate. Feminists, recognising the power

59 Casey Miller and Kate Swift, *The Handbook of Non-Sexist Writing*, 2nd edn (London: The Women's Press, 1988), introduction.

60 Stephen Kanfer, 'Sispeak' *Time* 23 October 1972.

of language to sustain structures and systems that treat women as inferior, work persistently for a change of language. Within the Christian churches some seek a reformation of sexism by calling for gender-inclusive language both for reference to the human as well as the divine. Inclusive language communicates new meaning in Scriptures and tradition and allows fresh revelations of truth hidden beneath centuries of male monotones. Indeed, one must question how public church discourse could possibly aspire to shaping Christian community unless the language used is just and inclusive. As biblical scholar Elisabeth Schüssler Fiorenza states: 'Sexism in theology is not so much a personal fault as a structural evil that distorts and corrupts theology and the Christian message.'[61]

The realisation that language is a powerful force in shaping social structures empowers those with a feminist consciousness to subvert church language. Unless we mutilate the male repository of language the fundamental perceptions of patriarchy will remain in place. However, the movement to inclusive language is a hard and complex journey. As we peel back the layers of sexism in language, we will discover that exclusive language also cloaks the prejudice of racism. Gradually we'll see that

> Inclusive language reflects that all people are full human beings with equal value and dignity; it avoids excluding, demeaning or stereotyping anyone on any basis; its personal images for God reflect analogously all humanity; without any favour to any.[62]

A truly inclusive language is not simply about men using male and female pronouns in their discourse, or finding a set of neutral and thus inoffensive alternatives. Cameron concludes that: 'Radical theorists remind us that there is no neutral language: the entire system since it belongs to and is controlled by men is permeated by sexism through and through.'[63] This brings me back to an earlier point: until women can share in the public

61 Elisabeth Schussler Fiorenza, 'Towards a Liberating and a Liberated Theology: Women Theologians and Feminist Theology in the USA,' in Jossua and Metz, eds, *Doing Theology in New Places*, Concilium 1155 (New York: Seabury, 1979), pp. 27–28.

62 National Council of Churches, USA, *An Inclusive-Language Lectionary Year A* (John Knox, Westminster and Pilgrim Presses, 1983–1986), p. 16.

63 Deborah Cameron, *Feminism and Linguistic Theory*, p. 91.

ordained discourse of their churches, sexism in language will remain. In other words, men reversing pronouns while clinging doggedly to exclusivist male power will do little to eradicate deep-rooted sexism. It is my deep belief that structures and systems of male domination will not be transformed until we *have a revolutionary change in the language we use, as well as change in the users of public language.*

Imagining a New Symbolic

The critique is clear. The question remains: how can we move beyond the 'rotted names' which do not reflect or respect our experience as women? How can we disrupt the monologic and allow both sexes to speak with different voices? Or, as Irigaray poses the question:

> How can we speak so as to escape from their compartments, their schemas, their distinctions and oppositions … Disengage ourselves alive from their concepts?[63]

The living creation of a new symbolic does not – cannot – take place with the patriarchs. Irigary reminds us that it cannot occur within the forum of 'their' distinctions and oppositions. I recall a conversation I had with a male cleric after I delivered a paper on 'The Feminist Critique of Language'. 'You must convince me,' he retorted trying to provoke me to answer his objections, 'for remember I am one of those who hold the power and can choose to change or not.'

The 'Disruptive Tactics' of Women

One of the first steps towards imagining new discourses incorporates what Irigaray names as 'disruptive tactics'. This is the creation of language which turns male monologic on its head through the use of laughter, playfulness and mimicry. Such tactics can be used as women talk to one another, especially within the context of small-group work, calling to mind examples of female exploitation by male discourse. Then, by using mimicry and playfulness, they convert this form of 'subordination into an affirmation'. By exposing the ridiculousness of male logic in its objectification of women, women are making 'visible' what was supposed to be invisible and ultimately rendering impotent the power of masculine monospeak.[64]

The use of metaphor and imagery is another 'disruptive tactic' proposed by Irigaray. We must 'overthrow syntax by suspending its eternally teleological order, by snipping the wires, cutting the current, breaking the circuits, switching the connections, by modifying continuity, alteration, frequency, intensity'.[65] Such imagery depicts the radical task ahead. If male dominance is to be subverted then we must jolt the present system and make new connections which will validate different discourses. Elsewhere Irigaray asks her readers 'to imagine a type of "short circuit" in the relation between subject and object, so that the object begins to speak and the subject is blown to pieces losing its previous hegemony'.[66]

While not accepting the violence of such imagery, one recognises that it jolts the imagination and challenges women. To short-circuit present laws of language would require women to refuse to participate in mixed company where men talk 90 per cent of the time.[67] Furthermore, women, in demanding the establishment of shared patterns of communication in both the public and the private sphere, would reject the male pattern to interrupt, contradict or mediate their words.

To engage in such 'disruptive tactics' women must live in a state of constant vigilance and critical awareness in relation to accepted modes of speech. The power of patriarchal language to constrict and constrain our lives must be challenged consistently and overthrown. Women must deliberately empower and encourage one another so as to create a new order of interactive and mutual exchange.

64 Luce Irigaray, *This Sex Which is not One*, p. 212.

65 Luce Irigaray, *This Sex Which is Not One*, p. 76.

66 Luce Irigaray, *The Speculum of the Other Woman*, p. 142.

67 Ofelia Schutte, 'Irigaray on the Problem of Subjectivity,' *Hypatia* Vol. 6, No. 2.

The Question of Silence

Silence, while often imposed on women, can also be chosen by women as a subversive tactic. Women often feel that they fall between the signs in the present symbolic system of representation. They sense that sometimes it is a waste of breath to speak as their words will simply be subsumed into the monotone of male discourse. In the interval, between all-male discourse and a mutual exchange between the sexes when communication will recognise and respect differences in language and speech, many women chose silence as a position of strength.

A film I viewed recently titled 'A Question of Silence' showed clearly that silence can be a 'source of an active transformative practice'.[68] The story is about three women on trial for the murder of a male boutique owner. Finding themselves interrogated within a patriarchal juridical system, these women choose the strategy of silence. A female psychiatrist, representing a different economic background to the women in the dock, is appointed to assist the accused. She stands for the 'liberated' woman, the 'working' woman, the woman who has achieved 'equality'.

Initially she pleads with the women to speak up, to defend themselves. Gradually, however, as she studies their lives she begins to see the parallels between their lives and her own. She recognises that they are all engulfed in an all-male meaning system which offers no resonance to the female voice. She becomes aware how often she too is silenced and controlled in life by her husband and colleagues.

At the end of the film when the judge, in all his pomp and ceremony, pronounces his condemnation of the women, they break their silence and burst into uproarious laughter. This strategy must surely be read as a further example of what Irigaray calls mimesis. The metamorphosis of the old order will only happen when the inadequacies of the order are brought into bold relief, using the technique of either sound or silence.

68 I would recommend Mary Crawford's new book. *Talking Difference: On Gender and Language* (London: Sage Publication, 1995). In her research she clearly unmasks male patterns to dominate social exchange.

Language of the Female

Tactics that disrupt the male monopolisation of language is one way forward; another must be the creation, by women and among women, of a language which respects the specificity of our lives. In other words, critique must be coupled with creative transformation of language. Just as women must grow into their own experience as women, so too we must grow into a discourse that is ours, one that is:

> adequate for our body, our sex, our imagination. It would be necessary for women to be recognised as bodies with sexual attributes desiring and uttering, and for men to discover the materiality of their bodies. There should no longer be this separation: sex/language on the one hand, body/matter on the other. Then perhaps another history would be possible.[69]

As women become subjects of their own speech, a new history will be born. The age of 'the proper', the generic, the neat and tidy definitions which ignore women's existence, will come to an end. Male monologic will dissolve into a sea of complexity and ambiguity. As Ducilla Cornell says, 'We'll have to dance differently with old distinctions.'[70] As the supressed and repressed elements of women's conscious and unconscious lives find active expression, a new poetics, a new style becomes mirrored in language. It is a style that gives figurative expression to the desires, the aspirations, the creativity of our own emotion/body/mind/spirit.

Luce Irigaray's own creative writings are a clear example of what this new language looks like. Her prose/poetry clearly employs a new syntax, a new representation which gives expression to her female specificity. Her work is indeed 'an attempt to define the characteristics of what differently sexualised language' looks like.[71] The contiguous, the diffuse, the fluid nature of her writings affronts us as strange only as long as we remain caught in the

69 In her book *Without a Word: Teaching Beyond Women's Silence*, Magda Gere Lewis examines the distinction between silence imposed on women and silence chosen as a tactic (Londin: Routledge, 1993).

70 Ducilla Cornell, *Beyond Accommodation*, p. 18.

71 Luce Irigaray, 'Women's Exile,' pp. 62, 76.

trajectory of the content and form of the male imaginary. I include some examples of such novel and powerful language of the female in Appendix A.

Female Poetics

Irigaray is not alone in giving us examples of what a female representation would look like. The Irish poet Eavan Bolan in her new book speaks as a woman poet of 'my own hesitant progress towards a voice that was mine'. She writes of the differences which open up when traditional elements are disassembled and women cease being objects 'eroticised and distanced' within male poetry.

> The woman poet is in that poignant place where the subject cannot forget her previous existence as object. There are aesthetic implications to this, but they are not separable from the ethical ones. The chief ethical implication it seems to me is that when a woman poet deals with these issues of the sexual and the erotic, the poem she writes is likely to have a new dimension. It can be an act of rescue rather than a strategy of possession.[72]

Boland's journey into her own subjectivity as a woman poet is a story filled with courage and a sense of ethical responsibility. She is consciously aware of the 'possibilities and subversions within poetry itself'. (p. 254)

In her quest for a language she can grow old in, a poem she can die in (p. 209) she realises that she must leave the certainties of her mind, a mind schooled in the conventions of male linguistics, and enter the questions of her own body as woman (p. 114). It becomes evident that stepping back into her body, claiming her bodiliness, is integral to reclaiming her voice and her vision. If what Emerson says is true, namely, that 'language is fossil-poetry', then it is surely in creating a new poetics faithful to our life and

72 Eavan Boland, *Object Lessons: The Life of the Woman and the Poet in Our Time* (Manchester: Carcanet Press, 1995), p. 215.

experience as women that we can free words and create a new possibility for language. We must above all recognise the body's imprint in language.

One of the most potent and fertile sources of a novel female poetics is the contemporary work of Irish women poets. Selected examples of such enticing and revealing language of the female 'imaginaire' can be found in Appendix B.

Imaging the New Symbolic: Visual Arts

The textual practice of poetry is clearly one site for the radical renewal of language.

Artistic expression within the visual arts is a powerful way to express such theory. *Sounding the Depths* was a collaborative installation by Pauline Cummins and Louise Walsh which was shown in the Irish Museum of Modem Art in 1992. Tired of feeling beleaguered as feminists and artists and refusing to be seen as 'the other', these women came together to re-present their lives, their bodies, as women. 'We are fed up trying to survive, only survive, instead of finding a space for all of us to thrive in', Walsh laments. 'We won't shut up. We'll not be silenced. We'll find the strength to open up.'[73]

The exhibition is a very powerful example of women finding their voice in finding their bodies. A new symbolic is imagined, rooted in the female body, and incorporating a plurality of expression in visual image, sound and words. Divided into three sections, the first set of images was mounted in a very small restricted room; these images depicted bodies in tension, clenched fists, tightly shut lips. Exhibited in a more expansive space, the second section images change and transition. Life returns to the bloodless lips, energy begins to flow, bodies relax. One of the images is an opening mouth projected on to a naked torso.

The final room is a celebration. Large images of women relaxed and open fill the area. The gaze is inward and outward, confident and happy.

73 *Object Lessons*, pp. 232–33.

Sounds of human laughter, gurgling water fill the air. Open mouths are superimposed on each woman's belly or chest, indicating that inner repression has been replaced with confident expression. Healed woman has returned to her body, her speech. Both the collaboration between the women artists in mounting this exhibition and the imagery of women within the installation are a subversion of the 'female model as passive' role. Here women as subjects of their lives, of their own sexuality, are choosing what images they wish to project and how they wish to give voice to the sound of their body and blood. Many of the images recall the ancient Irish image of the Sile Na Gig, an icon of open female sexuality portrayed with its gaping vagina.[74]

In this work artists Cummins and Walsh have decided to return 'to the country of the body'. Gazing out from that site, they speak their minds. Their imagery reinforces the point that only insofar as we rediscover our corporeal sexuality will we, as women, find speech. The courage, the boldness of this exhibition recalls Nuala Ni Dhomhnaill's words:

> We are damned, my sisters, we who swam at night on beaches, with the stars laughing at us phosphorescence about us we shrieking with delight with the coldness of the tide.[75]

74 See notes published by the Irish Museum of Modem Art to accompany the exhibition *Sounding the Depths* 1 April–9 May 1992. My commentary on the exhibition has been helped by Moira Roth's notes in this collection.

75 An excellent documentation on the origins and function of Sheela-na-Gigs can be found in Eamonn P. Kelly's book of the same title, published by the National Museum of Ireland, 1996.

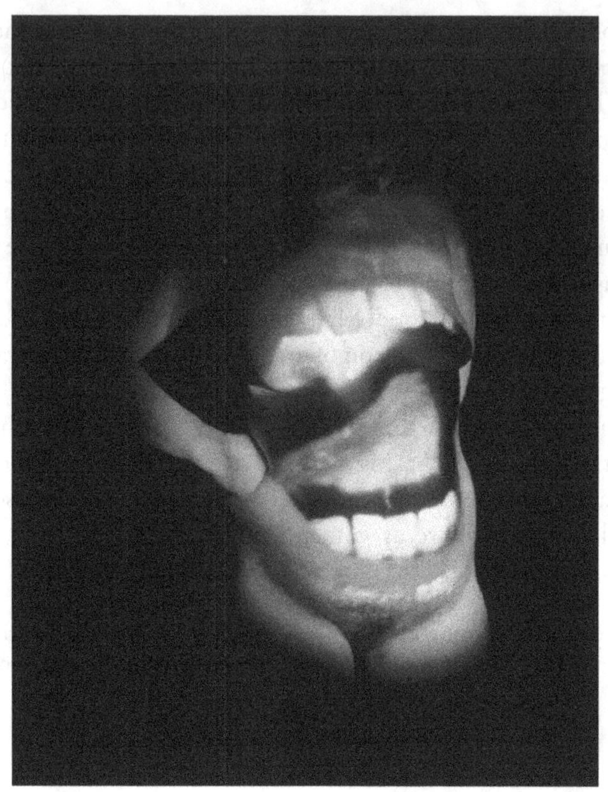

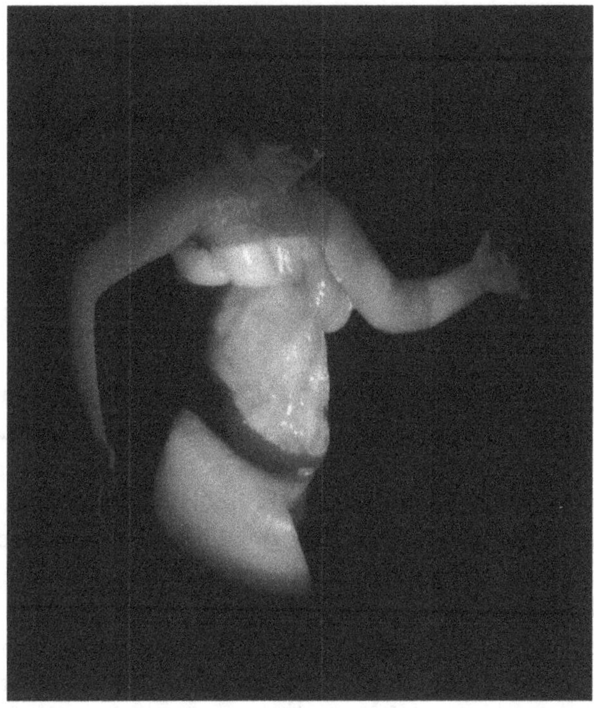

The Wickedary: Birthsite for Women's Words

Another extraordinary example of creative eruption of women's words is Mary Daly's work, especially as exemplified in *Webster's First New Intergalactic Wickedary of the English Language*.[76] Cleverly intertwining scholarship, rage and humour, Daly summonses words from their imprisonment in the silent background of patriarchal existence to re-establish

76 Nuala Ni Dhomhnaill, *Selected Poems*, trans. by Michael Hartnett (Dublin: Rave Arts Press, 1988).

them in the foreground of female becoming. She weaves and spins new 'word-webs'. Her *Wickedary* shakes the foundations of the all-male world of definition and description. As cracks appear in the faltering edifice of conventional usage, she encourages women to fill the gaps, the blank spaces, with their creative words.

The Female Language of Women's Spirituality

Another place where the new poetics of a female imagination is being voiced is within women's spirituality groups throughout the world. I have witnessed rituals created and conducted by women for women in places as diverse as Latin America, Australia, Europe and the United States. It would seem that once they come into their own, women are 'ideologically freer' to create occasions of deep spiritual meaning and insight. Dislodging their energy for a critique of institutions that refuse to listen, more and more women are creating their own ritual communities, sharing a Word that heals and empowers. I am convinced that this is a world movement of spiritual renewal, a movement where the female imagination is finding public symbolic expression. The plurality and diversity, the complexity and ambiguity, the richness and beauty which finds expression in women's rituals holds a hope for the regeneration of the universe. We are crossing over a new threshold. Hopefully the change that is erupting can be attended to with love.

Conclusion

Throughout this chapter I have claimed that integral to the establishment of female subjectivity is the symbolic representation of that identity in a new and living language. For this creative language to faithfully and publicly express femaleness – including female sexuality and female desire – it must be rooted in a female imagination. To break women's silence means to awaken the female imagination, for it will be the symbolisation of the female imagination that will move us towards a new order. As part of the birthing process into this new paradigm we must critically and creatively examine our language and the imagery of the divine.

As women give expression to a female language in all its diversity and integrity, they are breaking the absolute claims of man-made language. They are engaging in a 'political resistance', refusing to be silenced, rejecting victimhood. Such acts of creative expression reflect Audre Lorde's resilience. 'I am not only a casualty, I am also a warrior.'[77,78] As we break from monoreality, let us place active trust in the extraordinary elasticity, complexity and creativity of language. There is a beauty in language that cannot be revealed in a sexist world. We must ban the lie of sexism and speak creatively of the truth of our lives.

77 In cahoots with Jane Caputi (Boston: Beacon Press, 1987).

78 Audre Lorde, *Sister Outsider, Essays and Speeches* (California: The Crossing Press. 1984), p. 41.

CHAPTER THREE

Divine Difference

> Imagine a dower of settle beds tumbled from heaven.
> Like some nonsensical vengeance come on the people,
> Then learn from that harmless barrage that whatever is given
> Can always be reimagined.
>
> Seamus Heaney, *The Settle Bed*[1]

In a world where the debate about the sacred and the secular has long been decided in favour of the secular, God-talk might seem an irrelevancy which reflects an archaic order. Yet the question of God continues to haunt post-modern consciousness and, contrary to expectation, it will not go away. Human conversation about God continues, although it lisps humbler truths about the divine reality. It is as if the longed-for horizon of meaning cannot be sated without the Other – calling, cajoling, challenging us forward.

While the question of God persists, finding language and imagery for our understanding of the Divine which resonates with the breadth of human experience is more difficult. In recent years the naming of divine reality has altered radically. There is an acceptance now that exclusive male imagery and symbolism for the divine has contributed little to establishing a world of equity and mutuality. While maleness has been affirmed in inherited God-language, femaleness has been suppressed, thus silencing a whole aspect of Divine being.

There is a piece missing in this critique, however. Furthermore, this piece provides an essential clue towards a way of reimagining divine reality which genuinely unleashes the creative and healing potential of female as well as male. This piece is a feminist understanding of 'sexual difference'.

1 *Seeing Things* (London: Faber and Faber, 1991), p. 29.

As I have outlined in previous chapters, sexual difference, imagined from a female embodiedness, is a metaphor which acknowledges the fundamental differences between maleness and femaleness, as well as a metaphor which invites mutual relations between males and females. However, it is based on the understanding that mutual relations can only be fashioned through a fundamental acknowledgement of the myriad differences between female and male subjectivity. Consequently, aspirations towards a new world of mutuality hinge on the representation of both male and female subjectivity in divinity. The exclusive oneness of representing 'men only' in divinity must be opened up so that alterity in harmony can be imaged in Holy Mystery. If the divine, as imaged and languaged by the human, has always shaped the construction of subjectivity and social systems, then the human aspiration for a world of mutuality will not be realised without divinity imaging mutuality within sexual difference.

Need for New Naming

The task of naming and imaging divinity in different ways is as important for the construction of a society beyond patriarchy, as it is for the survival of religion. If, for example, the official voice of the Roman Catholic Church persists in the exclusive naming of God as 'he' or 'Father' in a world where growing numbers of men and women are aware of the injustice of sexism and are striving to live relationships of mutuality, then this religious tradition will be deemed irrelevant and will die. The survival of any religion is dependent on its ability to interpret present experience in meaningful fashion. Elizabeth Johnson puts the idea even more forthrightly: 'If the idea of God does not keep pace with developing reality, the power of experience pulls people on and God dies, fading from memory.'[2]

2 *She Who Is: The Mystery of God in Feminist Theological Discourse* (New York: Crossroad, 1992), p. 15.

Towards New Anthropological Foundations

To talk of the divine in a constructive way – in a way that really promotes the mutual potential of female and male – requires firstly that we build new anthropological foundations. Anthropological understandings articulated within patriarchy have always accepted the normativity of the male human being. The challenge to women – and men – is to disentangle the human from the masculine and allow women's self-representation to become visible. The way the human is understood affects the way we order reality on earth and in heaven. To have grown accustomed to male normativity, to have accepted without question maleness as the universal construct, has damaged not only female self-image, for she is always represented as inferior in such a framework, but it has also distorted our entire conception of reality.

Theological anthropology has been firmly rooted in patriarchal perceptions of male superiority. As I indicated in the previous chapter, the study of the interpretations of the Imago Dei concept since the early Fathers reveals this fact. Men are capable of reflecting the divine image in ways women are not. It is interesting that in recent Roman Catholic Church documents such as *Mulieras Dignitatem*, written in a climate where blatant sexism is becoming less acceptable, male and female equivalence in the Imago Dei is postulated as if this were always Church teaching. However, despite the apparent modernity in understanding, this has not led to the Church's retraction of the 1978 Vatican declaration which deems that women cannot be ordained as they are 'ontologically' incapable of imaging Christ.[3] In fact in the recent Apostolic letter from Pope John Paul II we are told that the ordination of women cannot even be discussed![4] And more recently we are told it is an infallible teaching.

3 See Rosemary Ruether, 'Imago Dei, Christian Tradition and Feminist Hermeneutics,' in *Image of God and Gender Models*, edited by Kari Borresen (Oslo: Solum Forlag, 1991), pp. 258–281.

4 John Paul II, 'Apostolic Letter on Ordination and Women,' *Origins* Vol. 24, No. 4 (9 June 1994).

There is great ambivalence today in a theological anthropology which on the one hand seeks to reflect current musings about equality, but on the other hand wishes to sustain structures which continue to exclude women at all the highest levels of power, decision-making and ordination. A theological anthropology of equivalence and mutuality will only find voice when the structures and lifestyle reflecting such equivalence are in place.

The way forward, as I have proposed, is to re-examine the notion of 'sexual difference'. It will be in the radical reinterpretation of the difference between males and females that a genuine possibility for mutual respect will be born. Furthermore, this reinterpretation will radically alter our understanding of the divine.

Divine Imagery of the Patriarchal Notion of Difference

> And God
> Reduced to a hostage among hostages.
>
> Muriel Rukeyser [5]

The presumption that the normative human being is male leads naturally to the conclusion that male imagery should be used for God. Indeed, the way we've imaged God has been one of the great stabilising forces of the oppressive 'sameness' that has marked our world. The way to be either God or human is male; anything different is inferior. A patriarchal understanding of 'sexual difference' has obliterated the possibility of equality and mutuality between men and women.

The genealogy of inherited Christian God imagery is exclusively male. Virtually nowhere in the lineage from heaven to earth does femaleness feature. Indeed the Council of Toledo of 675 spoke of the Son as being born out of the Father's womb:

5 'Letter to the Front', © Muriel Rukeyser from *The Collected Poems of Muriel Rukeyser*, 2005, University of Pittsburgh Press, by permission of William L. Rukeyser.

> We must believe that the Son was not made out of nothing, nor out of some substance or other, but from the womb of the Father (*de utero Paths*), that is that he was begotten or born (*genitus vel natus*) from the Father's own being.[6]

And Aquinas lamented the impossibility of Motherhood being used in God imagery because God is an active agent, not passive, which, according to Aquinas, is the foundation upon which Motherhood rests.

The imagination that has framed traditional God imagery has been male. Patriarchal sameness has been promoted and sustained by this inherited God imagery and sexual difference has been disregarded. Indeed, the power base upon which patriarchy rests would crumble if a feminist understanding of sexual difference was recognised. All-male imagery for the divine which has shaped the public religious imagination for centuries promoted a male ideological base. With this strong backdrop, it is easy for men to act on the stage of life as if all power is rightfully theirs. Put simply, fathers have benefited from a religious tradition soaked in Father imagery and sons have been exalted by the same tradition. The promotion of one sex in God imagery camouflages the real differences between men and women and reduces humanity to the One, the male, the God. This reductionist fascination with Oneness obliterates the plurality of experience and the dipolar reality of much of the human as well as the natural world.

Oneness: A Reductionist Concept

An understanding of sexual difference, where both female and male subjectivities are viewed as mutually different yet mutually related, suddenly throws into question our inherited fascination with Oneness. The construction of Oneness has benefited maleness, has exalted the one human being, the male, on high, so high he and God are indistinguishable.

6 As quoted by Janet Martin Soskice, 'Can a Feminist Call God "Father"?', in *Speaking the Christian God: The Holy Trinity and the Challenge of Feminism*, ed. Alvin F. Kimel, Jr. (Michigan: Eerdman's Publishing Company, 1992), p. 93.

Furthermore, I would claim this construction of Oneness, or the imaging of monotheism, is directly linked to the destruction of sexual difference. It is well known that Hebraic monotheism came to birth as a counterpoint to the many fertility religions with multiple Goddesses. This fascination with Oneness is a further example, if one is needed, that patriarchal theology is not imaged from a neutral, asexual base but rather is impregnated with the masculine notion of bodiliness.

Patriarchal Notions of Difference Breed Dualisms

The failure of divine imagery to embrace a positive understanding of difference, above all sexual difference, has been one of the cornerstones of dualistic thinking. Dualistic thinking elevates the One over and against the Other. It splits reality and exalts certain attributes, while negating their opposite. Placed at the top of the patriarchal pyramid, the One God resides over layers of dualisms. This God is imaged as strength, as Life, as Light. Weakness, death and darkness have no place in 'him'.[7] Maleness is imaged and projected onto this pinnacle of perfection. Femaleness is 'other' which is ascribed as deficient in dualistic thinking, representing all that God and man are not.

The Non-relational One

This one-sided being, which patriarchy has imaged in its own likeness and called 'God', is devoid of emotion and therefore non-relational. This is

7 I am aware that my focus is on the Jewish-Christian image of an all-male, all good-God. As David Lemming illustrates in his biography of God, the male God has many cultural embodiments in different religions and myths. He reminds us that one group's religion is another's mythology. See D. Lemming & J. Page, *Myths of the Male Divine God* (Oxford: Oxford University Press, 1996), pp. 3–7.

especially true when God is described as the 'unmoved mover' and other such metaphysical designations. Many of us can remember St Thomas' five proofs for the existence of God. While the logic is impeccable, this promising weave of reason unravelled when it came to relating emotionally to this Omnipotent, Omnipresent God. This non-relational God reigns easily over a social system where individualism is prized and greed rewarded. Indeed, monotheism effects an ordering in politics, especially the politics of blatant self- interest, which must be redressed. In short, patriarchal monotheism promotes masculinity and just as patriarchal projections of masculinity are harmful to men, so too I would suggest that divine imagery of the patriarchal notion of difference is destructive of the Divine.

A relational understanding of divinity must be prefaced, however, by the praxis of 'mutual relationship between men and women'. Therefore, it is dependent on the lived subjectivities of sexual difference. Catherine Keller puts it clearly: 'Philosophically and theologically, a radical monism or monotheism too easily tempts us away from a truly multiple integrity.'[8] Such 'multiple integrity' will never be realised without recognition of sexual difference. As I have shown, radical monotheism acts as a shield against taking such difference seriously.

From Living Image to Static Idol

The failure to recognise plurality in harmony within divinity, or multifaceted unity, has allowed the images of monotheism to slip from being living image to becoming static idol. The determination to preserve oneness and maleness closes off all ambiguity; the metaphor dies and solidifies into the equation that Fatherhood and God are one. The mystery of divinity is lost in such clarity. Ruether reminds us: 'It is idolatrous to make males more "like God" than females. It is blasphemous to use the

8 Keller, *From a Broken Web*, p. 181.

image and the name of the Holy to justify patriarchal domination … The image of God as predominantly male is fundamentally idolatrous.'[9]

Our inherited monosyllabic imagery for 'God' has created a social and religious worldview that is not simply oppressive of women and nature but also of men and of divinity. The critique is clearly in place. The time to move on is now. Gradually the backdrop which supported Classical Theism is crumbling. The feminist and womanist vision, ecological consciousness, new scientific understandings and process philosophy are all chipping away at the static monolith of monotheism.

However, we must recognise that change 'will come dropping slow'. (Yeats). We must be vigilant against the cheap co-optation of inclusive imagery in certain Christian traditions. Today some public Church services alternate Father with Mother imagery and certain school texts have started to remove the sexist God imagery contained therein. However, where such happenings take place in institutions which rigidly preserve patriarchal systems and which continue to exclude women from the hierarchies of power, proclaiming this to be 'the will of the Father', I must simply conclude that the language of feminism is being appropriated to make religious patriarchy more palatable. I would question the liberal agenda being called to titillate the unchanged Male God with some feminine accretions. The liberal temptation to collapse difference into an equality of sameness simply camouflages an unaltered patriarchal system. Women must remain constantly vigilant and expose this lie of change, demonstrating that 'inclusive language' rings false within exclusivist structures. Image breaking and image making are both profoundly complex processes. It will take far more than bending a few words to uncover the underlay of unchanging sameness.

Divine Difference Reimagined

Having lived with a cultural and religious tradition that deems difference as either 'less than' or 'same as' (thus, obliterating it), there is an

9 Ruether, *Sexism and God-Talk*, p. 23.

extraordinary challenge to the imagination of our age to re-enter and re-interpret this notion of difference as 'different and mutual'. It is my conviction that the redemption of God from the vestiges of patriarchy and the creation of a social order of mutuality between men and women is dependent on this new understanding of sexual difference.

As I have shown, when Irigaray speaks about sexual difference she means the irreducible difference between the sexes. Here difference is treated in non-dichotomising ways; the claim that women are different from men does not mean that they are better than or less than, but simply that they are different. In the first chapter, I made clear that the challenge to women is to find and articulate themselves as subjects of their own existence. However, the religions of the West have done little to foster or support the development of female subjectivity. As Irigaray reminds us:

> We have no female trinity. But as long as woman lacks a divine made in her image she cannot establish her subjectivity or achieve a goal of her own. She lacks an ideal that would be her goal or path in becoming … If she is to become woman, if she is to accomplish her female subjectivity, woman needs a god who is a figure for the perfection of her subjectivity.[10]

The question must now be addressed: how can this God of men become an image to inspire both male and female subjectivity?

In the second chapter, I proposed that once born, subjectivity must find symbolic expression, which in turn must impact public discourse. In this chapter, I will show that this journey for women, beyond the gaze of male expectation of who she ought to be, towards fashioning the subject of her own becoming, is not achievable without radically critiquing our inherited religious imagery and beliefs. This is especially important if one agrees, as I do, 'that the basic values, myths and rituals of any civilisation are in fact its religion'.[11]

The exclusivist male imagery of God has been one of the strongest social forces to confirm women in submissive roles and self-abnegating postures. Put more strongly, I would submit that 'Good old God' (as Lacan spoke

10 Irigaray, *Sexes and Genealogies*, trans. by Gillian C. Gill, pp. 63–64.

11 Grace M. Jantzen, 'What's the Difference? Knowledge and Gender in (Post) Modern Philosophy of Religion', *Religious Studies* 32 (1996), p. 446.

of him) imagery is the foundation stone upholding phallocentric societal structures. As Irigaray says,

> Man is able to exist because God helps him to define his gender (gendre), helps him orient his finiteness by reference to infinity …
>
> In order to become, it is essential to have a gender or an essence as horizon. [M]an has sought out a unique male God. God has been created out of man's gender. [12]

Western religion has taken divinity away from women and has legitimated an understanding of female power as impotent. Males have grown to manhood projecting the infinity of maleness onto divinity, while females have been robbed of such a horizon. Again, Irigaray reminds women:

> Divinity is what we need to become free, autonomous, sovereign. No human subjectivity, no human society has ever been established without the help of the divine … If women have no God, they are unable either to communicate or commune with one another.[13]

The exhortation of Christian theology has been that we must grow in the image of God. But if God is male, women are simply left with the option of becoming an image of man and fulfilling male desires. Irigaray is not defending traditional religious beliefs and practices in her use of traditional categories. However, as a psychoanalyst and philosopher influenced by Nietzsche and Feuerbach, she is clear about the important place of God imagery on the horizon of human becoming. As she states, to achieve our essence both women and men 'must imagine a God …

12 Irigaray,, 'Divine Woman', in *Sexes and Genealogies* (New York: Columbia University Press, 1993), p. 61.

13 Ibid., p. 62. It is important to note here that, as psychoanalyst and philosopher, Irigaray refuses to let go of the notion of God or the divine. She holds onto this idea not in any overt religious sense but because of its potential catalyst in women's search for self. The potential of a divine ideal on the horizon of female becoming can be seen in the power Father God has had in sustaining a society of structured male dominance. For further elaboration on Irigaray's understanding of the divine see Elizabeth Grosz's article, in *Transfigurations: Theology and the French Feminists*, ed. by C. W. Maggie Kim et al. (Minneapolis: Fortress Press, 1993), pp. 199–214.

Only the religious within and without us is fundamental enough to allow us to discover, affirm, achieve certain ends'.[14]

Imaging the divine as the horizon of female and male becoming, where difference not sameness is celebrated, would expand the vistas of human potential in ways thus far unknown. Imaging gender difference in non-dichotomising ways, where femaleness would no longer just represent the flesh, and maleness the mind, would radically alter our dualistic image of the Divine. Imagery of a masculine God, who identifies simply with matters of the mind, would no longer resonate as true. The challenge is to put bodiliness back into divinity, to find divinity in our own flesh, and then to articulate the sexual difference of both maleness and femaleness into the symbolic order of divine naming.

Although the reconstitution of God imagery/God language is not an easy task, feminist theologians, philosophers and spiritual mentors must continue to be courageous midwives of this new tradition. In a world of growing apathy and easy atheism, where people feel alienated by outmoded articulations of religious meaning, the fallow ground of spiritual yearning could be cultivated anew. It is of the essence that we assist towards the birthing of a living language for divinity, a language that affirms sexual difference.

To speak of 'God' is to take an imaginative, a conceptual leap. It is to speak of the unspeakable. As Kristeva reminds us: 'God resides in a gap.'[15] A break exists between the infinite and the finite which in our idol-making tendency we have failed to respect. We dissolve the infinite in finite solutions. We have divested divinity of infinity. The way forward is to find living metaphors which stretch and pull between the 'is' and the 'is not', metaphors which, like the imagination which created them, crack and strain for ever new namings which might 'lisp the truth' of divine reality.

When God Dies …

The heritage of male imagery for the divine reflects a history of men trusting confidently in their own experience and placing on the horizon

14 Irigaray, *Sexes and Genealogies*, p. 67.

15 Julia Kristeva, 'Stabat Mater' in *Tales of Love*, p. 261.

of their male-becoming a divine presence ever calling them forward, ever stretching their potential. The man-made divine male affirmed and boosted the identity of human maleness. Just as women should critique the male religious propensity for imaging God in their own likeness, they should also be suspicious of the modern male cry that 'God is dead'. This is simply the other side of the same mirror. For when males kill the male god they fill the vacuum by themselves becoming gods. Nietzche alludes to this in the words of the mad man:

> Whither is God?… I will tell you. We have killed him – you and I.
>
> All of us are his murderers. But how did we do this? How did we drink up the sea? Who gave us the sponge to wipe away the entire horizon?… Is not the greatness of this deed too great for us? Must we not ourselves become gods simply to appear worthy of it?[16]

Atheism in a phallocentric world is no solution. It simply clears the stage for unbridled maleness. As the male god dies, all males become gods. While I critique and reject the exclusivity of these traditions and the oppressive manner in which they have been used to support male superiority, I affirm the placing of sexual imagery in divinity.

Women's Difference as a Resource for Divine Imagery

It is time now to re-represent sexual difference in divinity. It is time for men to return in a humbler vein to cull their experience for imagery of divinity that will enable them to live a new identity- one of mutual partnership with women and with the earth. It is time for women, for the first time in the Jewish-Christian tradition and many of the other world religions, to place their experience of difference at the centre of the inquiry for new divine imagery.

Mary O'Reilly de Brun, in her recent analysis of images and metaphors for God articulated by a group of Irish women, shows that women

16 Friedrich Nietzche, *The Gay Science*, trans. Walter Kaufmann (New York: Vintage, 1974), p. 181.

have begun to trust their own experience of the divine.[17] She posits that women, in their movement from 'silence to sacred speech', are producing 'three distinct though interrelated patterns of metaphorical speech':

- nature-based metaphors
- metaphors of the 'ineffable'
- female metaphors.[18]

I will simply take one example from each category in order to illustrate the newness of this discourse about divinity.

Nature-Based Metaphors

> God is a presence. It's white, like a white cloud. A beautiful wrapped-around thing, a serenity deep inside me, something that never goes away. I can sink into the cloud, yet I can get out of it easily. A cloud with the sun shining through, the heat of the sun. I feel absolute bliss there. The heat of the sun, that's very strong. If I stop and think about it, the cloud is more Spirit than anything. (Thelma, p. 183)

There is an interweave of immanence and transcendence here which dissolves the old dichotomies that wedged separation and distinction between the God above and the earth below. The Spirit moves easily through this woman's experience and in that movement there is a bonding, an intimacy that empowers above all with a feeling of *jouissance*.

Metaphor of the 'Ineffable'

In the second classification of responses, women expressed enormous reserve, indeed reluctance, to name the unnameable.

17 Mary O'Reilly de Brun, *From Silence to Sacred Speech: An Exploration in Feminist Spirituality* (MA thesis for Maynooth, 1992).

18 Ibid., p. 81.

> I don't want to reduce the enormity of God to manageable little symbols, neatly packaged, domesticated harmless God. I think the glimpses I've had of it over the years are of stillness and you know that kind of silence after the music ends, after the words end. I think the reality of God, whatever that means, is terrifying newness really. (Alison, p.185)

The 'terrifying newness' reflects not only the reality of God but also the vistas into the unknown now opened up by women listening and attending to their experience as women.

Female Metaphors

In the research sample the majority of women spoke of God using female imagery. This signifies a new coming to birth of the divine female and the female divine. It is clear that when women image divinity as female they find a corresponding ease in claiming their own subjectivity, their own identity as women.

> There's that line in that [book] you know, to find God in myself and to love her fiercely; that is really a sentence that stopped me in my tracks. Like there didn't seem to be any way to find God as a woman unless you stopped being a victim, unless you stopped being powerless or unless you reclaimed your power, unless you pull yourself out of victim situations. And you can follow that through on a lot of levels. (Alison, p.160)

There is a radical shift in this naming and imagery of the divine. There is both a psychological and a social dimension clearly in evidence. In naming the divine out of female experience, women are affirming and touching an inner potential and strength, hitherto untapped. Birthing new imagery for the Sacred from the depth of their femaleness is a deeply spiritual experience for women. New images and symbols are not forced or imposed but arise out of a new relationship with the divine. The movement is from stillness to meditation to open receptivity.

Women's spirituality groups are a central source of where individual insights are ritualised and celebrated. In such moments of bonding, the community of women recognise that we are members one of another and together we can and will effect change.

As new religious images and symbols emerge from the reflected experience of women's lives, it is vital that this sacred speech is heard as an emancipatory discourse in the public arena. To effect the transformation of the oppressive symbol system which we have inherited, women must proclaim publicly their inspired insights into divine naming, and insist that exclusivist structures change to reflect female language.

Divine Metaphors Irrupting from the Female Experience of Sexual Difference

The Mother Image

Motherhood is surely one function women can claim as exemplifying their sexual difference and could therefore be culled as a resource for imagery for the divine. Indeed, some might anticipate that as women delve into their own experience for images of the divine they would find consolation and empowerment in the image of God as Mother. Yet it is interesting to note that few of the Irish women surveyed put forward this image as helpful. Their silence indicated that at best motherhood is a mixed metaphor.

The Christian feminist movement has sought in recent years to bring to the foreground the Scriptural foundation for this image. The retrieval of this atypical tradition reveals an underside to Scripture where maternal imagery was used for the divine. For example, Dorothee Solle reminds us: 'The most important image the Bible uses for God's pain in the world is an image from the experience of women, the image of giving birth.'[19] However, it must be clearly noted that this tradition seldom found voice and was never used to empower the maternal within the public discourse

19 *In Gustavo Guiterrez's Honour*, p. 330.

or to shape the social order. This is not surprising as there was no underlying structure to hold or promote the female or female-oriented images.

Furthermore, in our own time, following twenty-five years of Christian feminist scholarship which has sought to restore this tradition to the public imagination, little change is evident. Indeed, it has had little impact on the official discourse of the patriarchal churches who have so controlled the interpretation of Scripture over the years that they have virtually obliterated from the religious imagination any possibility of imaging the divine in female form even in our present time.

The problem, however, is broader than this and rests in the very construal of motherhood itself within patriarchy. A 'mother image' for divinity which is rooted in the patriarchal notion of difference is extremely problematic. Julia Kristeva reminds us that 'we need a new discourse on motherhood, one that liberates the logic of the maternal body and that in so doing is creative of new and more mobile subjective and cultural identities'.[20] We must liberate motherhood from the domestic and private sphere where it has been housed and controlled by the culture of male dominance.

This will entail questioning the patterns of parenting we have grown to accept. As long as women as mothers are abandoned by the economic logic of male society to the role of primary parent, relationships of mutuality and reciprocity between men and women are impossible. Fostering the patriarchal myth that mothers hold the primary responsibility for the nurture of children also promotes detrimental relationships between women and their children.

Freud's theory of the Oedipus Complex is a hypothesis about the boy child's need for separation from the mother in order to achieve ego identity. This extremely male analysis is rooted in the premise that mothers are and ought to be the primary parent. Freud's conclusions suggest that boy children, in order to develop, feel the need to dramatically escape from the clutches of their mothers and thereafter live with a deep fear of ever really bonding with women again. Standing back from such a theory, we

20 As quoted in Phyllis H. Kaminski's essay, 'Kristevas and the Cross: Rereading the Symbol of Redemption,' in *Women and Theology*, eds, Mary Ann Hinsdale and Phyllis H. Kaminski (New York: Orbis Books, 1995), p. 236.

can only conclude that the patterns of motherhood imposed by patriarchal acculturation are the breeding ground for a sexist and heterosexist society.

This same culture blocks the development of the mother-daughter relationship. In her book, *Jocasta's Children*, Christiane Olivier examines the relational lack between mothers and their daughters.[21] This 'lack', fostered within present familial structures, promotes tension among and between women in later life. Luce Irigaray interprets the mother-daughter problematic within patriarchy as rooted in the lack of separation between them: 'There is no possibility whatsoever, within the current logic of sociocultural operations for a daughter to situate herself with respect to her mother: because strictly speaking, they make neither one nor two, neither has a name, meaning, sex of her own, neither can be identified with respect to the other.'[22] Furthermore, the failure of the mother to be a self enrages the daughter: 'I received from you only your obliviousness of yourself.'[23] The complete selflessness that patriarchy has honoured in mothers leaves many daughters guilty and angry that they must follow suit. Irigaray voices it in this way: 'And what I wanted from you mother was this: that in giving me life you still remain alive.'[24]

If patriarchy is perpetuated by female complicity in their own oppression, this is nowhere more evident than in the mother-daughter relationship. Many mothers glimpse an alternative, see a way of living beyond the conventions and norms of male-centred existence. However, the fear of being different dissipates their courage and frequently results in daughters being exhorted to love, honour and obey, the ways things are. To enter the relationships of a phallocentred world, mothers implicitly teach their daughters that they must give up an authentic relationship with themselves and live in focused fulfilment of male needs. In her study of daughters, Carol Gilligan found that as girl children entered adolescence they experienced a sort of 'psychological foot-binding'. Suddenly their earlier

21 Chnstiane Olivier, *Jocasta's Children: The Imprint of the Mother* (London: Routledge, 1989).

22 Luce Irigaray, *This Sex Which is not One*, trans. Catherine Portcner with Carolyn Burke (Ithaca: Cornell University Press, 1985), p. 143.

23 *Ibid.*, p. 65.

24 *Ibid.*, p. 67.

courage, resilience and openness shut down as if they became aware of the cost of the compromise that lay ahead.[25]

If women as mothers are the primary initiators of their daughters into the mores of patriarchal existence, they could also be the ones to break this cycle and instigate patterns of dissonance. Such countercultural acts of resistance would have to be sustained by group process work, both for the mothers themselves and for mothers and daughters together. Working recently with a group of Traveller women in Tallaght, Dublin, I was brought face to face with the difficulty of this task. The women had come through many months of personal development work and could name how oppressive their lives as young women had been. After the Catholic ceremony of Confirmation, at twelve, they had been taken out of school and given no freedom. They were then obligated to work always by their mothers' side in a domestic context. The fear that permeated this custom was that they might lose their virginity, bring disgrace on their families and ultimately be rejected by suitable Traveller men. They simply moved from the enslavement of young adolescence to the imprisonment of marriage where they were considered the male's property. Although these women were clear about the difficulty of their lives as girls and now as mothers, they were insisting that their daughters must follow a similar path.

Sexless Mary – Meek and Mild

A further domestication of the mother's power is found in the traditional Marian symbol within Catholic Christianity. Mary, imaged as virgin *and* mother, renders invisible the desire, the bodiliness of real women. Sexuality is reduced to the level of innuendo. The sexless maternal virgin promotes a sanitised image, far removed from the ebb and flow, the natural rhythms of female existence. Any call to mothers to be women in their own right challenges the whole tradition and symbolism of the

25 Lyn Mikel Brown and Carol Gilligan, *Meeting at the Crossroads: Women's Psychology and Girl's Development* (Cambridge: Harvard University Press, 1992), p. 218.

virgin mother. Also, the image of the Virgin Mary symbolises the absorption of the female by the mother. Father God needs the womb of woman to bring his Son into the world. In other words, the Christian tradition does not honour femaleness, but rather woman in her role as mother. Olivier concludes: 'It is within maternity, not sexuality, that the main inequity between the sexes lies.'[26]

References to Mary, the mother of Jesus, are brief and rare in the Christian scriptures. The words from the original text portray a prophetic woman who in the Magnificat speaks of her defiance, her stance against oppression. The images of this woman from these early accounts are equally courageous: she stood by Jesus on the cross. Yet the doctrines which sprung up around her life effaced her real presence and quickly made her a paragon of femininity. The one-sided portrait of her meekness and humility bears little resemblance to the young Nazarene woman who said yes to the mystery of life.[27]

Motherhood Revisited

We have seen why the image of 'divine motherhood', if situated within the patriarchal notion of difference, does not empower women's discovery of their subjectivity and creative potential. Neither does it emancipate the divinity from 'oneness' and 'sameness'. However, I suggest that the metaphor still holds possibilities for the incorporation of sexual difference in divinity. As Julia Kristeva reminds us:

26 Olivier, p. 137.

27 Jaroslov Pelikan in his recent book, *Mary Through the Centuries: Her Place in the History of Culture*, draws our attention to how the Latin Vulgate translated, or really mistranslated her words in the Magnificat: 'Quia respexit humilitatem cincillae suae' (Luke 1:48 Vg), p. 221. Pelikan chronicles the history through the centuries of the development of devotion and doctrine of Mary. It is fascinating to see how depictions of Mary in the bits and pieces of Scripture were elaborated into full-blown doctrines often providing negative symbols of women.

> There might doubtless be a way to approach the dark area motherhood constitutes for a woman; one needs to listen more carefully than ever, to what mothers are saying today.[28]

If we engage in a 'severer listening' (Adrienne Rich) to the changing role of motherhood, we could hear emerging a discourse on motherhood articulated from the creative centre of women's lives. Freed from patriarchal impositions of a sacrificial motherhood, which leaves the woman for dead, a woman-identified discourse could formulate the potential power of this role for women who freely choose it. Indeed, Helene Cixous, in her text 'The Laugh of the Medusa', proposes that women's reclaiming of motherhood is an integral component to their reclaiming of their bodies, their voices, their subjectivity, in a word – their difference.[29] She posits:

> There is hidden and always ready in woman the source; the locus for the other. The mother too is a metaphor. It is necessary and sufficient that the best of herself be given to woman by another woman for her to be able to love herself and return in love the body that was 'born' to her.[30]

In naming motherhood as their own, women could touch anew the creative source from which they birth and nourish. This reclamation of motherhood by mothers themselves could allow their expression of womanhood to be a well, nourishing a deep self-love and self-affirmation. Giving birth could be a moment of new becoming, nurturing bonds of mutual love. Therefore, motherhood could be a liberative image for the divine and for women and men, as long as the understandings of motherhood underpinning the image are articulated as part of a female discourse. Mary O'Reilly de Brun's research allows us to hear what such a discourse sounds like:

28 Stabat Mater, p. 179.

29 Helene Cixous, 'The Laugh of the Medusa,' trans. K. & P. Cohen, *Signs* 1/1 (1976): 875–899.

30 Ibid., p. 881. I would highly recommend Gerardine Meaney's analysis of Cixous' work in her book *(Un) Like Subjects: Women, Theory, Fiction* (London: Routledge, 1993), pp. 15–51.

> I was praying, calling on God in some way for guidance or help or something. I can't explain what happened really, I was just admiring the sunset, a very blood-red sky, and feeling drawn into it, when I understood that this was God, everything was God's womb, and I was in there waiting to be born. And once I knew that I knew I was already born of God, I had come from God's womb, I was still in God's womb and I would return to God's womb. It was the most complete feeling, renewal. (Adrienne, p.67)

Allowing sexual difference to infuse divine imagery opens up dimensions of Holy Mystery that have been camouflaged for too long. Entering the 'womb of God' and being entered by holy mystery intimates a physicality to divine relationality that metaphysical abstractions have lost. Furthermore, such relational understanding calls into question the rift we have inherited between transcendence and immanence. As one enters 'the womb of God' immanence intersects with transcendence. The intimate embrace of love in the womb of God opens to a sense of completeness. The wonder, the Otherness of holy mystery is understood in the depths of intimacy and nearness. Luce Irigaray suggests, and I agree, 'Perhaps we are passing through an era when time must re deploy space? A new morning of and for the world? A remaking of immanence and transcendence, notably through this threshold which has never been examined as such: the female sex.'[31]

When imagery of the Divine as Mother arises out of the discourse of women and is not idealised or sanitised by patriarchal projection, it opens up understanding of God's pain, God's vulnerability, which have been silenced up to this. A relational God, imaged as woman in childbirth, is a God who feels, who suffers with the pain of the universe. It is to this vulnerable God we can turn for healing.

It is important to recall that our search for new metaphors and images for the divine is to enable sexual difference to shatter the cast of patriarchal idols which have imprisoned holy mystery and disempowered women. This said, it is equally important that we accept that no single metaphor will or should attempt to contain the divine. Restoring the discourse of

31 *The Ethics of Sexual Difference,* Trans. by Carolyn Burke and Gillian C. Gill (New York: Cornell University Press, 1993) p. 18.

motherhood to women and encouraging women to plumb the depth of this experience for divine resonances is but one among many images with potential for empowerment. Nor does such imagery exclude the retrieval of Father imagery for divinity. In fact, exploring the notion of sexual difference encourages such diversity. The challenge will be to shift the imagination from Father as idol to Father as metaphor, one among many for the divine.

Goddess Imagery

Another metaphor for the divine which is re-emerging, as women touch the complexity of their experience, is Goddess. As women dive deep within their own spirited bodies they are drawn backwards to the ancient roots of their experience. The evoking of the ancient memory from matrilineal times, that God once was a woman, that the divine was always imaged in female metaphors, frees the imagination from its patriarchal moorings. Such excavations into the past are not expressions of nostalgia for times long ago, rather they are political acts that can empower women and affirm that which is female in the present. Carol Christ makes the point well:

> When I first said the word Goddess, I experienced my own being in the image of God(dess) in a new way. The word Goddess was for me an important affirmation of the legitimacy and beneficence of female power, of the goodness and beauty of women's bodies and their connection to nature, of the validity of the female will, and of the importance of female-female bonds.[32]

The return of the Goddess as an empowering symbol in women's spiritual quest tells us something about symbols. Although 'symbols arise from the unconscious' and 'die if they hold little cultural relevance', they can return if the community and cultural context become favourable.[33] The eruption

32 Carol P. Christ, *Laughter of Aphrodite: Reflections on a Journey to the Goddess* (San Francisco: Harper & Row Publishers, 1987), p. 66.

33 Katherine Zappone, *The Hope for Wholeness: A Spirituality for Feminists* (Mystic, CT: Twenty- Third Publications, 1991), p. 93. I highly recommend Zappone's careful analysis of symbols, images and metaphors in her chapter, In the Presence of the Sacred'.

of Goddess imagery in this present time loosens the grip of exclusively male symbolism upon the contemporary imagination and indicates that the culture of patriarchal monotheism is cracking and the divine female is visible in the fissures.[34] This very imagery also allows us to realise that Goddess symbolism never entirely died and indeed in Celtic cultures was never too far from the surface. Folklorist Dáithí Ó hÓgain once told of an old and pious Catholic woman in County Limerick who described to him the burial of her husband as a going into the hill to be with Domhain, the old Celtic Earth Goddess.[35]

The work of Marija Gimbutas shows clearly that in Old Europe (6500–3500 BC), the sacred and the secular interwove, allowing spirituality to permeate all existence. In this period of egalitarian relationships, people lived in harmony with nature and one another. This ancient civilisation was different because then women were respected and the Goddess was worshipped as the primary religious symbol:

> The Goddess in all her manifestations was a symbol of the unity of all life in Nature. Her power was in water and stone, in tomb and cave, in animals and birds, snakes and fish, hills, trees, and flowers. Hence the holistic and mythopoeic perception of the sacredness and mystery of all there is on Earth.[36]

In her archaeological excavations, Gimbutas has unearthed thousands of female figures. The religious interpretation of many of these symbols is warranted because they were located at the sites of cult or ritual ceremonies and also in burial tombs.[37]

Both Irigaray's work on 'Divine Women' and Gimbutas' work on the ancient female religious symbol of the Goddess provide a language and an imagery that enable the dismantling of the male sky god. We now shift

34 See also David Lemming and Jake Page, *Myths and the Female Divine* (Oxford: Oxford University Press, 1994).

35 This story was remembered by Professor Sean Freyne.

36 Marija Gimbutas, *The Language of the Goddess* (San Francisco: Harper & Row, 1989), p. 321.

37 The *Journal of Feminist Studies in Religion* (Fall 1996, Vol. 12, No. 2) has dedicated an issue to the legacy of Marija Gimbutas who died on 2 February 1994 after a life of committed and imaginative scholarship.

our gaze from the heavens to the earth, and hope for new imaginings and namings of the divine.

All women will not be comfortable with Goddess language or goddess imagery initially. Opening to the strange, to the other, reconnects the self to ancient roots from which we have been severed for too long. Such reconnection with the past feeds our imagination in the present and presents new possibilities for the future. As Patrick Kavanagh says: 'On the stem of memory imagination blossoms.'

As women reconnect with the female in the divine, they will honour the divine in the female and affirm female ways of being. The restoration of female symbolism for the Sacred will gradually unravel a social fabric of exclusive male control. As the female principle re-emerges in divinity, a new cultural concern for the matrix of the earth and the health of all the planet will unfold. I am arguing that this process is *essential*, though not necessarily done by all women, if the Sacred is to effect the power of mutual love within our world. However, we must be forewarned that this is radical work and will be perceived as such. In 'jamming the discursive machinery',[38] which sustains an all-male God, in reinstating from a past carefully buried the presence of a female divine, we are engaging in a dangerous task. If talk of 'difference' is silenced in a world of patriarchal sameness, then intimations of divine difference will unleash the most vehement censorship.

This God Which Is Not One

It is important to clarify, as many feminist theologians, theologians and others have done, that talk of the Goddess does not imply a single fixed transcendent being outside woman but rather 'the self-affirming be-ing in women'.[39] Goddess talk implies diversity, pluralism, complexity – a break with static oneness that has reduced divinity to maleness. As Luce Irigaray states: 'The very word goddess, in fact, always seems to have the

38 Irigaray, 'The Power of Discourse,' in *This Sex Which is Not One*, trans. Catherine Porter with Carolyn Burke (Ithaca: Cornell University Press, 1985), p. 78.

39 Mary Daly, *Gyn/Ecology*, p. 111. See also Susan Thistlethwaite. *Sex, Race & God: Christian Feminism in Black and White* (New York: Crossroad, 1989), p. 123.

implication of one of many, not one unique one. For centuries the One has remained entrusted to God, even though this longing for the unique is a specifically male nostalgia.'[40]

In prising open understandings of diversity in divinity, goddess imagery recalls a polytheistic past when male and/or female imagery was equivalent. The Neolithic period leaves us a memory which must not be obscured. There once was a time where males and females shaped a social structure which was non-hierarchical and where power was mutually shared. I believe this matrilineal period was profoundly influenced by the fact that divinity was imaged in diversity, that sexual difference was represented in holy mystery. The reawakening of Goddess symbolism in our time will hopefully push against our intolerance for diversity, and allow us to recall the essentially plural character of ultimate reality.

It is interesting to note that a growing number of feminist theologians today are questioning our inherited tradition of the 'Simple One', which for Catherine Keller promotes 'competitive exclusivism … stifles the imagination and so kills image at the source'.[41] In her search for a God-language that respects the need for diversity, complexity and relationality, Mary Hunt recommends the metaphor of the 'divine as friends'.

> Perhaps the most suggestive image that emerges out of women's friendships is not one divinity but many. Just as friends do not exist in the singular, neither is it feasible to imagine that something as complex and comprehensive as divinity could be singular either.[42]

Such polytheistic proposals jolt the imagination and call into question the static monotheism male dominance has imposed on divinity. The effect of shifting the ground under the accepted imagery for divinity is to create a clearing in the imagination for new symbols and metaphors and images of holy mystery. This is an opportunity for theology to become a more human discourse, a time to ensure that 'the fullness of female humanity

40 Irigaray, *Ethics of Sexual Difference*, trans. by Carolyn Burke and Gillian C. Gill (New York: Cornell University Press, 1993), pp. 68–69.

41 *From a Broken Web: Separation, Sexism, and Self* (Boston: Beacon Press, 1986), p. 249.

42 Mary Hunt, p. 167.

as well as male humanity and cosmic reality serve as divine symbol in equivalent ways.'[43]

Love as Sacred Metaphor

In calling for the inclusion of sexual difference in divinity, I have proposed the retrieval of female metaphors such as 'motherhood', or metaphors which open to diversity and pluralism such as 'Goddess'. However, the metaphor which holds most promise, I believe, is that of divine love. The Johannine statement that 'God is Love' (1 John 4:16) is one of the most powerful statements of the Christian scriptures. To speak of God as love is to recognise that love constitutes divine existence. Love is the very being of God. As Catherine Mowry LaCugna states so well, 'Love causes God to be who God is.'[44] This is a metaphor which has lain dormant, however, in a patriarchal tradition which has imposed images of male domination and metaphysical abstraction on divinity. The authoritarian patriarch exalted by this male-centred tradition has existed in solitary isolation, far removed from the relational understanding of love.

Not only has patriarchy robbed us of any appreciation of relational love in the heavens, it has also distorted our experience of love on earth. The autonomous self, the separate self is promoted far more than understandings of the relational self. Rampant individualism and cut-throat competitiveness are the values that permeate our society. As I have already indicated, patriarchy breeds distorted relationships between women and men, and between parents and children. As long as women remain trapped in the patriarchal image of who they ought to be, their capacity to love shrinks, shrivels to be contained by man-sized proportions and expectations. The confining domestic environment that economic dependency dictates, stifles the infinite horizon of female becoming, of female loving. Catherine Keller describes this state as 'relational entrapment' which women accept because

43 Elizabeth Johnson, p. 47.

44 Catherine Mowry LaCugna, *God For Us: The Trinity and Christian Life* (New York: HarperCollins, 1991), p. 261.

of 'the gilded promise of love',[45] a promise which, of course, can never be fulfilled. The ethic of selfless devotion, which women have bought into for so long, robs the female capacity for mutual relation and ultimately leads to stagnation in male-female relationships. Put simply, loss of self ultimately leads to loss of the capacity to love.

The reality of divine love will only filter into the imaginations of women and men today insofar as they relearn their infinite capacities to love, freed from patriarchal constraint.

A social construct which opens up an appreciation of sexual difference would break the cast of independent males defending their separate selves, afraid of or avoiding love, and dependent females living selfless lives. 'If the *one* of love is ever to be achieved, we have to discover the *two*.'[46] Women and men must discover their unique capacities to love differently, for it is this difference that will enhance and enable mutual relationship. Our call to live lives of love in mutual relation, which as Carter Hayward reminds us is synonymous with living lives of justice,[47] is rooted in and sustained by the Sacred who is love. The relational metaphor of 'divine love' is thus unearthed and revitalised through women's and men's search for subjectivity embodied in the affirmation of sexual difference.

The equation of the divine with love, as love, was evidenced in the earlier Hebrew Scriptures, most notably in the Song of Songs. This beautiful poem where the Sacred and the sexual co-mingle, where body and soul conjoin, is a love song intoned in harmony. Gregory of Nyssa notes the passion of this love song and here interprets it as the erotic relationship between the divine and the human:

> The bride then pulls the veil from her eyes and with pure vision sees the ineffable beauty of her spouse. And thus she is wounded by a spiritual and fiery dart of desire (eros). For love (agape) that is strained to intensity is called desire (eros) [48]

45 Keller, *From a Broken Web*, p. 17.

46 Irigaray, *An Ethics of Sexual Difference*, p. 64.

47 *Touching our Strength: The Erotic as Power and the Love of God* (San Francisco: Harper & Row, 1989), p. 3.

48 Gregory of Nyssa's Commentary on the Canticle (p. 44, 1048): English text in Musurillo, from Glory to Glory as quoted in Catherine Mowiy LaCugna, *God For Us*, p. 352.

This reflection links desire and God and reconnects the divine with woman in a relationship of amorous intent. The intensity of love flowing through the Song of Songs reminds us that the flame of love is eternal and will not be quenched by death.

> Love no flood can quench no torrents drown.
>
> *Song of Songs* 8:7

Therefore the God who is love, loves us not simply out of selfless concern or dutiful charity as agape is so often depicted, but rather out of a plenitude, a passion that stretches beyond God's self. Again Catherine Mowry LaCugna is correct:

> The God who is Love does not remain locked up in the splendid isolation of self-love but spills over into what is other than God, giving birth to creation and history.[49]

The ethical implication of imaging divine love in this way is to challenge the one in love to stretch out beyond himself or herself towards a creative expression of that love. This often is concretised in the creation of a common unity where this abundance can be shared. If faithful to the Christian vision, such a community must embrace and partner with those who have few resources in life.

Divine Diversity

To accept the full implication of the statement 'God is Love' is to accept that the primary ontological category for the divine is relation, 'in the beginning is the relation'.[50] Although a male monotheism has permeated our imaginations with an image of an isolated deity given to authoritarian

49 LaCugna, p. 355.

50 Martin Buber, *I and Thou*, trans. by Walter Kaufman (New York: Charles Scribner's Sons, 1970), p. 69.

individualism, such ideology distorts the tradition. Augustine in De Trinitate presented the Trinity in relational imagery; the divine persons live rooted in a community of mutual relations. While feminists will wish to exorcise the exclusively masculine imagery imposed on this tradition, many agree that Trinitarian understandings of the divine hold promise. For in this image,

> God is figured not simply as a singular subject but as a community of persons in mutual relation where both substantive difference and fluid exchange constitute a Divine being who is at once self-contained and radically open to relation.[51]

Carter Heyward proposes three images that would sustain a relational appreciation of the divine: 'God is our relational matrix (or womb). God is born in our relational matrix. God is becoming our relational matrix.'[52]

In an early article, moral theologian Margaret Farley proposed that the mutual relations within the divine community which is the Trinity could be a foundational image for fostering egalitarian relationships between human beings.[53] Each divine person is both active and receptive in the interchange of love. In imaging such interpersonal communion, stereotypes of masculine activity and feminine passivity in patriarchal patterns of relationship would dissolve and both sexes would be challenged to be 'actively receptive' in all loving encounters. Relationships between females and females, males and males would also honour such principles of mutual loving respect.

Such imagery takes seriously the radical relationality at the heart of divinity, named as love. Just as such imagery opens up understandings of divine becoming in the infinite possibilities of our loving, so too it reminds us that it is only in loving that we will savour the divine.

Made in the image of love, the essence of human becoming is to grow in the capacity to live in love. It is love that allows us to live heaven on earth; it is love that conjoins heaven to earth. In loving we will come to know

51 As quoted by Serene Jones in her article, 'Divining Women: Irigaray and Feminist Theologies,' *Another Look: Another Woman*, Yale French Studies 87 (1995), p. 62.

52 Heyward, *Touching Our Strength*, p. 24.

53 Margaret Farley, 'New Patterns of Relationship. Beginnings of a Moral Revolution', *Theological Studies* 1975. pp. 627–646.

and understand the shape of a new world order where harmony and mutuality reside. Luce Irigaray reminds us that 'our destiny is … to generate the divine in us and between us.'[54] Our search for God imagery is above all a search for imagery that will jolt the imagination towards the praxis of love. A new imaginative picture of the relationship between God and the world will precede action for a world of mutual justice. Re-imagining God is a vital component in the process of living an ethics of emancipation. The litmus test for the truth of any image of the divine is the praxis of human community which it inspires. It is therefore my belief that amazing revelations about divine reality would follow if we begin to take seriously and image in our praxis, the reality of sexual difference. In other words, if we once really respected the other in our midst then maybe we could grasp something about the otherness of the divine. In accepting difference in our midst we will be more able to let go fearlessly into mystery, which is surely the journey, the meaning of life.

To re-examine the metaphor 'God is Love' in light of the category of sexual difference is to push against any romanticisation or 'insipid vulgarisation of Christian love'.[55] It is to open the metaphor to the diversity, the otherness of Love. If human love is the coming together of difference, an experience of relationality where the other as other is respected and affirmed, then this experience opens up in entirely new ways the profound mystery, the radical otherness, of the divine who is Love. Until we recognise sexual difference we cannot recognise God in love or therefore truly understand our naming of God as Love.

Conclusion

Mutual relationships rooted in a respect and appreciation of sexual difference can, I would suggest, open the horizon of our understanding of life's deepest mysteries. But to accept the divine as Love, to image the divine

54 Irigary, *Divine Women*, p. 3.

55 Kristeva, *Tales of Love*, p. 161.

in love, is above all an act of imagination. Imagination is the site where ultimate reality is known. Insights from reason or revelation about the divine are always mediated through imagination. New symbols for holy mystery are first intimated in the imagination. Imagination is the rainbow which mediates between the human and the divine. To know divine mystery as love calls for an imagination that is moulded by love. To this we now turn.

CHAPTER FOUR

Towards a Feminist Imagination

> Could we not say by anticipation that imagination is the emergence of conceptual meaning through the interplay between sameness and difference?
>
> – Paul Ricoeur[1]

One of my foundational propositions is this: if the insights of feminism related to subjectivity, language and divinity are to mould a practice radical enough to change our world, imagination is the key. Imagination is the faculty which enables us to see the world in a new way; it is also the faculty which motivates us to act for the promise of the possible.

So it is time we asked – what is imagination? How can we articulate an integrated philosophy of its nature and activity? At the same time we must consider – how is our understanding of this faculty of the human person affected by the insights of feminism? In order to answer these questions, I examine first how imagination has been understood in the past. I argue that it is important to start by pointing to the reality of the 'pre-historic' imagination. There are significant clues during this period for our contemporary concerns. Second, I offer a feminist analysis of the philosophical history of imagination. I show how the philosophy of imagination – even as developed within a patriarchal framework of reality – contains elements that can be retrieved and brought forward in reshaping what imagination could be, namely, an imagination that shapes our being as well as our knowing. Third, I turn to the unfolding of the *female imaginaire*, as developed within the writings of Luce Irigaray. Here we see that an acknowledgement of the reality of sexual difference provides the essential starting point for the birth of a female imagination.

1 Paul Ricoeur, 'Creativity in Language', trans. David Pellauer, *Philosophy Today 17* (Summer 1973), p. 109.

These are the key building blocks, I believe, for the construction of a feminist imagination. Feminism is the political catalyst that encourages the birth of a female imagination that could take an equal standing within the space of public expression and discourse alongside the male imagination. It is a feminist eye that debunks the primary assumption of a patriarchal imagination that a male image of the world is normative and singular. It is therefore a feminist imagination that sparks the redefinition of 'imagination' to encompass female and male images of reality, and it is a feminist imagination which views the possibility of a world transformed by actions that are shaped by the acknowledgement of sexual and other forms of difference.

The Pre-historic Imagination

The usual starting point for the philosophical history of imagination is the Classical Greek period – more precisely the works of Plato. Reference is seldom made to the existence of this faculty in the 'pre-historic' period. Yet an examination of the numerous artefacts from the Neolithic era reveals that imagination was alive and well between 6,800 and 3,200 BCE, and found expression in richly creative imagery. The works of Marija Gimbutas document carefully that in Old Europe there existed a civilisation where agricultural communities grouped and gave imaginative interpretation to their lives using various art forms.[2] The survival of imagery from this period speaks of a cultural imagination that was inclusive in its understanding of both divinity and humanity. The Goddess was worshipped as the primary deity and reality was interpreted through the 'language of the Goddess'. This was a matrifocal society; there was no male dominance and no war. It would seem that before the dawn of Patriarchy women and men lived in a non-stratified society. Artefacts from the period tell us that these relationships reflected harmony in

2 Marija Gimbutas. *Language of the Goddess* (San Franciso: Harper & Row. 1989).

diversity. Burial patterns show that women and men were respected as equals. Europe's earliest cultural layers show evidence of an active female and male imagination, which found expression in manifold aesthetic and artistic achievements.[3]

If the imagination is the key faculty which allows us hold diversity in harmony, difference in unity, then it is hardly surprising that the dawn of patriarchy and its obsession with sameness, with oneness (maleness) and with hierarchies built on dualisms, would suppress this faculty.

The lopsided patriarchal promotion of maleness has not simply unbalanced all reality, but has extinguished a creative energy evidenced in this 'pre-historic' time.

3 In her work Gimbutas delineates the distinctions between the matristic Old European and the later patriarchal Indo-European systems. At the beginning of her life of scholarship, using an interdisciplinary method which combined archaeology and mythology (archeomythology), Gimbutas put forward 'proposals' which questioned the hegemony of patriarchy since the beginning of time. After forty years of research having unearthed thousands of artifacts which supported her thesis she was convinced that once there was a 'matrifocal' society which worshipped the Goddess and which probably was 'matrilineal' – tracing its ancestry through the female line. The evidence she unearthed provides a symbolic language which can be read. A language open to interpretation, yes, but no less reliable than the 'written' history which follows. This period ended by the invasion of Indo-European nations from the volga steppes in the East. Many of Gimbutas' findings were contested in the early years, however there is now a large body of scholarship both in archaeology and linguistics which support her paradigm. In recent years the work of Stanford University geneticist Luigi Cavalli-Storza has discovered genetic evidence supporting Gimbutas' thesis of an Indo-European invasion. Marija Gimbuas offers a new interpretative framework from which to understand the period of Old Europe. If we acknowledge this material '(it) may affect our vision of the past as well as our sense of potential for the present and future. We must refocus our collective memory. The necessity for this has never been greater as we discover that the path of "progress" is extinguishing the very condition for life on earth'. Gimbutas, *The Civilization of the Goddess: The World of Old Europe*, ed. Joan Marler (San Francisco: HarperSaaan Francisco, 1991), p. viii.

A Feminist Analysis of the Philosophical History of Imagination

In examining the history of the philosophy of the imagination from Plato to Paul Ricoeur, my intent is not to offer a comprehensive analysis of each of the key thinkers down through the centuries. This work has already been done.[4] Rather, my purpose in selecting certain authors has been twofold. First, I wish to highlight significant landmarks in the suppression and rejection of this faculty. Rooted in the fear that this faculty – if given free reign – would loosen the patriarchal grip on structures held together by the elevation of the rational, imagination was suppressed. The rejection of imagination was also linked to the equation of this faculty with the feminine. Sustaining male dominance was dependent on men's divorce from the 'feminine' side of their nature, represented by bodiliness, fluidity and fantasy. Second, in choosing certain philosophers and reading their works through a feminist lens, I have highlighted the potential of various insights from these thinkers. These can be retrieved in a present

4 The literature on imagination is vast. The following works have influenced the understanding of imagination presented here: Eva T. H. Brann, *The World of the Imagination: Sum and Substance* (Savage, MD: Rowman & Littlefield Publishers, 1991; Edward S. Casey, *Imagining: A Phenomenological Study* (Bloomington: Indiana University Press, 1976); Patricia Cook, ed., *Philosophical Imagination and Cultural Memory* (Durham: Duke University Press, 1993); James Engell, *The Creative Imagination: Enlightenment to Romanticism* (Cambridge: Harvard University Press, 1981); Mark Johnson, *Moral Imagination: Implications of Cognitive Science for Ethics* (Chicago: The University of Chicago Press, 1993); Richard Kearney, *The Wake of Imagination* (London: Hutchinson, 1988); Richard Kearney, *Poetics of Imagining: From Husserl to Lyotard* (London: HarperCollins Academic, 1991) Leonard Lawlor, *Imagination and Change: The Difference Between the Thought of Ricoeur and Derrida* (Albany: State University of New York Press, 1992 John McIntyre, *Faith Theology and Imagination* (Edinburgh: The Handsel Press, 1987); Paul Ricoeur, *The Rule of Metaphor: Multi-disciplinary studies of the creation of meaning in language* (London: Routledge & Kegan Paul, 1978); Mary Wamock, *Imagination* (London: Faber and Faber, 1976); Gerard Watson, *Phantasia in Classical Thought* (Galway: Galway University Press, 1988); Alan R. White, *The Language of Imagination* (Oxford: Basil Blackwell, 1990).

day articulation of the importance of this faculty for creating a new world and new ways of being in the world.

Plato: The Diminishment of the Imagination

As we move from matrilineal to patriarchal time – or, from myth to philosophy as Plato claimed many centuries later (427–347 BCE) – there is little surprise that imagination falls from favour. In The Republic, the earliest of Plato's dialogues (382 BCE), imagination is relegated to the lowest form of knowledge.[5] Plato images knowledge as a line divided into four parts; he places imagination and its sole capacity to imitate and often to deceive, at the opposite pole to reason. Reason alone has the capacity to know pure form and it is through reason that one can know God.[6] That is, it is the rational that allows us to know ideas, pure form and ultimately God. Phantasia (the Greek word for imagination) belongs to the order of sense perception, judgement and opinion. The imagination is that which allows us to know the material world, the world of the senses. The world of imagery and imitation is far removed from the world of pure form, original creation and is therefore riddled with illusion …

Again using an image, Plato compares humans condemned to this state of phantasia, to prisoners in a cave. The prisoners are chained to the floor of the cave facing the back wall. Images of moving objects are cast onto this wall from an invisible fire at the opening end of the cave. The prisoners take these images for reality. The challenge, according to Plato, is to free these prisoners (humans abandoned to the world of sense perception and opinion) and to bring them out into the light. In this way, they are introduced to the world of reason and knowledge of pure form which lies outside the body and the senses. It is clear that Plato's understanding and condemnation of phantasia is rooted in a dualistic worldview, a hallmark

5 Plato, *The Republic*. Translated with an introduction by A. D. Lindsay (London: J. M. Dent & Sons Ltd.).

6 *The Republic Book VI* (510 & IT), p. 204.

of patriarchy. In his worldview there is the world of Being and the lesser world of becoming. The world of Being is the unchanging world of forms, ideas and essences, known by reason alone. The world of becoming is in constant flux, condemned to bodiliness and deluded into believing that images are real. For Plato, to know is to transcend reality and to be inspired by bodiless forms. It is evident that Plato's epistemology is rooted in a repression of bodiliness, of matter and ipso facto of women.

Although Plato, in this earlier work, would see imagination as the poor relation of reason and perceives imaginative productions such as myths and images as belonging to the infancy of intelligence, his own epistemology is constantly exemplified by imagery. Indeed he produced some of the most memorable images in European philosophy as Iris Murdoch reminds us:

> Cave, the charioteer, the cunning homeless Eros, the Demiurge cutting the Anima Mundi into strips and stretching it out crosswise. He kept emphasising the imageless remoteness of the Good, yet kept returning in his exposition to the most elaborate uses of art.[7]

It must be stated that Plato is not alone among patriarchal philosophers who, while they discount imagination, illustrate their theories imaginatively. Michele Le Doeuff speaks about this 'as philosophy's own surreptitious traffickings in the world of images.'[8]

Plato's early mistrust of imagination is interrelated to his fear of the arts. His condemnation of poetry in general and Homer in particular commences in Book III of *The Republic* and reaches a climax in *Book X* with this outburst:

> Like one who gives a city over into the hands of villains, and destroys the better citizens, so we shall say that the imitative poet likewise implants an evil constitution in the soul of each individual; he gratifies the foolish element in it, that which cannot

7 Iris Murdoch, *The Fire and the Sun: Why Plato Banished the Artists* (London: Oxford University Press, 1977), p. 87.

8 Michele Le Doeuff, *The Philosophical Imaginary* (London: The Athlone Press Ltd., 1989), p. vii.

> distinguish between great and small but thinks that the same things are sometimes great and sometimes small, and he manufactures images very far removed from the truth.[9]

Here we see that poetry is found guilty of falseness. Born of the imagination, it simply imitates life and thus can lead one astray. It evokes an emotive rather than a rational state and thus must be feared. This denunciation of poetry is extended to all of the arts and in Book X Plato furthers this critique. He argues that the arts communicate untruths and traffic in deceit. They serve no useful purpose; they cannot illumine reality as they are but imitations of reality. This reproach of poetry as mere imitation stands in stark contrast to Audre Lorde's words:

> We must constantly encourage ourselves and each other to attempt the heretical actions that our dreams imply, and so many of our old ideas disparage. In the forefront of our move toward change, there is only poetry to hint at possibility made real.[10]

Plato's condemnation of the arts and relegation of imagination to the wings of our mental activity is a means of sustaining his world view. Perhaps his fear of imagination and its expression in various art forms was rooted in an intuition that the dualism and hierarchies of his epistemology would crumble if the integrative faculty of imagination was freed. Furthermore poetry's 'hint(ing) at possibility' would disrupt his static patriarchal order.

In fairness it must be mentioned that in some of his later dialogues such as the *Sophist* and the *Timaeus* Plato did modify his position slightly. In the *Philebus*, for example, imagination shifts from its representation simply in the order of becoming and finds a place in the order of being. Here the imagination has the capacity to 'paint pictures on the soul.' This hints at the potential of the imaginative faculty to know the order of being and pure form. Such imagery elevates the imagination beyond its earlier

9 Plato, *The Republic*, trans. and with introduction by A. D. Lindsay (London: J. M. Dent & Sons), pp. 308–09.

10 Audre Lorde, 'Poetry is Not a Luxury' in her *Sister Outsider: Essays and Speeches* (Freedom, CA: Crossing Press, 1984), pp. 38–39.

status, however, it remains a faculty that must always be subjected to the rigours of reason.[11]

Plato, imprisoned in a dualistic worldview, cannot fully affirm imagination. Yet amidst his fear of imagination and its affects, he does purport that knowledge of the sensible, material world is dependent on the imagination. However, in his hierarchical schema of knowledge he consistently places phantasia on the lowest rung of the epistemological ladder.

Aristotle: The Imagination as a Distinct Faculty

A reading of *De Anima* allows us to conclude that for Aristotle, just as for Plato before him, intellect reigns supreme.[12] Like Plato, Aristotle's treatment of imagination is filled with ambiguity, paradox and contradiction. Echoing fears from the past, Aristotle notes the error-prone nature of imagination stating that 'imaginings are for the most part false'.[13] Unlike Plato, however, Aristotle does not place imagination at the bottom of the epistemological ladder. Rather he moves it up a few rungs situating it between sense perception and reason. Although distinct from perception and reason – 'phantasia is different from perception and from thought'[14] – Aristotle sees imagination as interrelated to both and in constant movement between both.[15] In fact, he argues that reason needs imagination as 'the soul never thinks without an image'.[16] Yet Aristotle

11 See Richard Kearney's excellent book. *The Wake of Imagination* (London: Hutchinson, 1988) for a development of these ideas, especially pp. 99–105.

12 *De Anima* III, 3 is Aristotle's main discussion of phantasia.

13 *De Anima* 428a 11.

14 *De Anima* 427 b 14–17.

15 See Book III, end of chapter 10. This image of imagination as movement between perception and reason I attribute to Gerard Watson, *Phantasia in Classical Thought*, p. 15.

16 *De Anima*, 432 a 14.

outlines how the imagination is dependent on perception as the existence of any image implies a prior perception.[17]

The placing of imagination as a bridge between perception and reason distinguishes Aristotle's appreciation of imagination from that of Plato.[18] It augments imagination as important for the knowing process, although Aristotle argues that the imaginative faculty never initiates thought. For Plato, as I indicated previously, imagination was simply a combining faculty, that is, it combines sense perception, opinion and judgement, which are all rooted in our knowledge of the world of experience or material reality. Aristotle's understanding of imagination as a distinct faculty between sense perception and reason, continues to root it firmly within bodiliness but also places it within the realm of consciousness. It is the imagination that carries sense perception to reason.

Furthermore, the whole notion of a movement between sense perception and reason creates an image of the imagination as an active, dynamic faculty and not simply a passive, receptive one. In naming imagination as distinct, he elevates this faculty to an identity of its own and in so doing augments the importance of imagination. While I am signalling a certain growth in appreciation of this faculty within Aristotle's works, it would also be true to say that imagination is far from liberated in the writings of this classical Greek philosopher.[19] However, as I will indicate later, certain intimations of the potential of imagination found in these works could themselves be freed towards the construction of a feminist imagination. A third strand from this early Greek period offers a more positive interpretation of imagination. The Stoics (300 BCE) who were from the materialist tradition gave *phantasia* a central place in the description of the process of human knowing.[20] They claimed that to think truthfully and to

17 *De Anima* AH b 16. Watson puts it well: 'Phantasia must then be involved in the mutation of sense- perception into phantasmata, which are then available for the activity of the intellective soul.' p. 27.

18 Richard Kearney in his treatment of Aristotle in the *Wake of the Imagination* uses the image of bridge to summarise the function of the faculty in this period. 'It is both a window on the world and a mirror in the mind.' See pp. 106–13.

19 See R. Kearney, ibid.

20 Gerard Watson, in *Phantasia In Classical Thought* (Galway University Press, 1988) alerted me to this point.

act creatively one needs imagination. Indeed I would argue that the early Stoa (e.g. Zeno, Cicero) were the precursors of early modern philosophy, namely empiricism. In this brief sketch of the philosophical history of imagination I will now leap forward to that period.

1711–1776

David Hume: Empiricism and Imagination

David Hume was a pivotal thinker in the eighteenth century who advanced the understanding of imagination beyond the transcendental epistemology of the early Greek period. Hume was an empiricist, that is, he claimed that knowing is rooted in the observation of external nature, and is based upon an analysis of that which is seen and felt. As an empiricist, he dissembled the scaffolding of transcendent knowledge which upheld Greek epistemology; he claimed that it is not possible to know through the intellect alone. Instead, the building blocks of human knowledge have their foundation in the material world of sense impressions.

> An impression first strikes upon the senses, and makes us perceive heat or cold, thirst or hunger, pleasure or pain of some kind or other. Of this impression there is a copy taken by the mind, which remains after the impression ceases; and this we call an idea.[21]

Hume argues, therefore, that imagination is central in the construction of the edifice of human knowing. We cannot know truth or reality without the imagination, because it is imagination that connects sense impressions and ideas. In *A Treatise of Human Nature*, he states that an idea is an 'image' of an impression.[22] But imagination is not simply a staid carrier of

21 Pt. 1. Sec 2; S-B, p. 7.

22 Hume, *A Treatise of Human Nature*, ed. L. A. Selby-Bigge (Oxford: Clarendon Press, 1967) T 1. 6. 20.22. 134–135, p. 10. p. 4. See Alan White's *The Language of Imagination* (London: Basil Blackwell, 1990), pp. 35–43 for a helpful development of Hume's connection of imagination with ideas and impressions.

reality from the outer to the inner eye, it is creative in the way it combines and ultimately presents original impressions. He writes of this appreciation of the creative potential of the imagination in the following way:

> Were ideas entirely loose and unconnected, chance alone would join them, and 'tis impossible the same simple ideas should fall regularly into complex ones (as they commonly do) without some bond of union among them, some associating quality, by which one idea naturally introduces the other.[23]

In identifying the creative capacity of imagination, Hume names and honours it as the most free of all faculties. As he states: 'Nothing is more free than that faculty.'[24] An image he uses to describe its freedom and creativity is: 'A galley (that is) put in motion by the oars, and carries on its course without any new impulse.'[25] Furthermore, the freedom of imagination gives it its moral impulse – what is 'plainly possible for the imagination, is possible to be'.[26] Edward Casey, in analysing this aspect of Hume's philosophy, writes: 'Nothing is more free because no other mental act is as capable of envisaging possibility in its purity and multiplicity. The autonomy of imagining is an autonomy of freely projecting and of freely contemplating a proliferation of pure possibility.'[27]

Another significant component of Hume's exposition on imagination is the link he makes between imagination and emotion. As previously outlined, Hume argues that imagination is the linking faculty between impressions and ideas. He adds to this the following proposition: passion or emotion is aroused depending on the vividness of the imagery which translates an impression into an idea. He says: 'It is remarkable that the imagination and affections have a close union together, and that nothing which affects the former can be entirely indifferent to the latter.'[28]

23 David Hume, *A Treatise of Human Nature*, Book I, Part I, Sec IV; Ed. L. A. Selby Bigge, p. 10.

24 *Ibid*, pp. 79–80;89.

25 SB, p. 198.

26 Hume, *Treatise*, p. 89.

27 E. Casey. *Imagining: A Phenomenological Study* (Indiana Unversity Press, 1979), p. 233.

28 David Hume, *Treatise (Of the Passions)* Book 2 Part III, Section 6.

In other words, Hume posits that those who image vividly feel deeply. The strength of one's thought or feeling on any matter is dependent on the vivacity of the image that shaped the thought or evoked the feeling in the first place.

There exists a significant moral implication that Hume draws from this relationship between emotion and imagination. This is the area of sympathy. Without imagination our capacity to feel with the other would be sadly bereft. Sympathy implies an interpretative ability which not only enables understanding of how another feels but which opens up the creative possibility to feel within oneself what the other is experiencing. Hume writes: 'Sympathy is the conversion of an idea into an impression by the force of imagination.'[29] Such identification is key to moral motivation. This involvement of the self in the feelings of another is due to a great effort of the imagination. This weaving of emotion with thought, this placing of imagination as central to both, is a new phenomena within the philosophical history of imagination. It opens up a new acceptance of this creative faculty. To quote Hume again: 'The memory, senses and understanding are therefore all of them founded on imagination or the vivacity of our ideas.'[30]

It is important, however, not to overstate Hume's appreciation of imagination. While on the one hand he acclaimed imagination's attributes, on the other he expressed reserve. Although claims of the freedom and the centrality of imagination punctuate his work, the freedom of the faculty is bound by the 'order and form of the original impression.'[31] A feminist reconstruction of imagination would seek to free Hume's theories from such bondage, otherwise we would be left with a faculty which could change the order and form of patriarchy but not its essence or substance.

29 Hume, *Treatise of Human Nature*, p. 427.

30 *Ibid.*, p. 265.

31 *Ibid*, p. 9.

1724–1804

Kant: Imagination and Creativity

The development in Kant's writings of the place of imagination in human knowing is rooted in his fundamental disagreement with Hume that all knowledge arises from experience alone. While Kant is open to the empirical emphasis on the importance of experience he believes that the creative imagination is not simply bound to data supplied from material reality. But he also disagrees with Plato that transcendental knowledge, the realm of ideas and pure form, resides outside the human subject in some realm where the good or God alone resides. Rather, Kant took transcendence out of the sky and placed it firmly within the knowing subject, or more specifically within the faculty of creative imagination.

In the first edition of the *Critique of Pure Reason*, he distinguishes two forms of imagination – the reproductive and the productive. The reproductive or empirical imagination operates very much according to Hume's understanding. It weaves a synthesis between sensory experience and understanding. This is an image forming faculty – a faculty which makes sense of the senses. It gives order, unity, shape and form to the manifold of experience.

The productive or transcendental imagination is, as the names suggest, a constructive or creative faculty. This faculty is the hidden root of all understanding, for it gives content to our thoughts. Kant says that imagination is 'a blind but indispensable function of the soul, without which we would have no knowledge whatsoever'.[32] But being a transcendental faculty it can make new syntheses out of material received. In Kant's work there is an autonomy, an independence accorded to this faculty which we have not encountered before. Thus it is the faculty which allows us to think new thoughts spontaneously. The independence, the spontaneity of the transcendental imagination is highlighted by Kant when he speaks of its

32 Immanuel Kant, 1st critique A78, B103.

'purposiveness without a purpose.' How this is so remains a mystery, but that this is so is a fact.

Part of the work of the transcendental imagination is to create schema. By this abstract image Kant wishes to convey the notion that it is the imagination that brings imagery to experience in order to render it intelligible to understanding. As Kant states:

> This schematism of our understanding (which is the same as imagination) in its application to appearance and their form is an art concealed in the depth of the human soul whose real modes of activity nature is hardly likely ever to allow us to discover, and to have open to our gaze.[33]

In inventing schemas the creative imagination brings together a synthesis of intellectual data and allows us to make connections between what would be otherwise disparate realities. 'This art concealed in the depth of the human soul' is also what enables us to make aesthetic judgements. In the *Critique of Judgement* Kant tells us that in matters of taste, of beauty, the imagination again is central. Working in harmony with the understanding of an experience or event is imagination, which places order on sense impressions and allows us to acclaim the beauty of a given experience.

If, as Kant proposes, imagination is at the root of putting order on our sense impressions and of giving content to our conceptual understandings of reality, then it is imagination that must shift if we are to shape reality differently or understand things in new ways. While the empirical or reproductive imagination may be wedded to and embedded in the cultural, customary ways of imagining humanity and divinity it can be educated by bringing before the senses new possibilities of perceiving reality. This is possible to achieve as Wittgenstein reminds, 'images are subject to the will.'[34] However, from Kant's analysis, it is with the transcendental imagination that our real hope for change lies. For this productive, active faculty

33 *Transcendental Deduction*. Quotations from Kant are taken from Norman Kemp Smith's translation (Macmillan, 1929) B. 181. Quoted by Mary Warnock, p. 32.

34 In Edward Casey, p. 197. Zettel, eds, G. E. Anscombe and G. H. Von Wright (Berkeley: University of California Press, 1967), sec.621.

has at the root of its nature the power to construct creatively new ways of knowing and being – it is the faculty by which we can 'frame to ourselves a new world'.[35]

Naming imagination as the power of the mind to create new worlds, and to hypothesise new ways of being, augments this faculty to a sphere of importance unknown before. However, we must not overclaim Kant's appreciation of imagination; in his writings the productive imagination never becomes an active autonomous faculty initiating creativity. Rather, 'image is a power of the mind for organising and vivifying ideas in accordance with a direction that is given to imagination'.[36] Once again, in the philosophical history of imagination, there exists a reticence to allow the radical creativity of imagination its full potential. I am suggesting that such reticence is a subtle attempt to place this faculty at the service of a worldview that does not perceive difference as normative.

Coleridge: Imagination and Re-creation

Although Coleridge was anticipated in the main tenets of his thought by German philosophers of the prior century, his originality lies in the attempt to understand the psychology of the imagination. Coleridge was both an imaginative poet and a critic of the poetic imagination. From his poetry and his personal writings (especially between the years 1797–1802), we inherit a legacy that allows us to broaden our understanding of the imagination. Certainly he was deeply influenced by the thought of Kant but his own creativity helped shift the epistemological trajectory from the perception of the knower as an impersonal spectator of objective knowledge to the knower as a self-aware participant in the process of knowing. He did this mainly through his appreciation of the emotions

35 Kant, *Critique of Judgement*, as quoted by Alan White, The Language of Imagination.

36 Ray Hart, *Unfinished Man and the Imagination: Toward An Ontology and a Rhetoric of Revelation* (New York: Herder & Herder, 1968), p. 319.

in imaginative knowing. Coleridge claims: 'My opinion is this: that deep thinking is attainable only by a man of deep feeling and that all truth is a species of revelation.'[37]

In 'Dejection – An Ode', a highly emotive poem written in 1802, Coleridge speaks of 'the shaping spirit of imagination' and sighs:

> I may not hope from outward forms to win
> The passion and the life, whose functions are within.'[38]

In this poem, Coleridge intimates a twofold understanding of the imagination: it is an inner power shaping from within and it is linked to feeling. Coleridge also forged a link between memory and imagination. Without the 'hooks and eyes of memory' we are enslaved to a one-dimensional present. However, it is imagination that gives memory meaning; he states 'imagination … the true inward creatrix, instantly out of the chaos of elements or shattered fragments of memory, puts together some form to fit it.'[39] One of the continuing mysteries of the dynamic life of imagination is why certain images erupt from our memory charged with emotion while others lie dormant, forgotten.

In the *Biographia Literaria* (published in 1817), Coleridge goes to great length to clarify his understanding of imagination.

> The imagination then, I consider either as primary, or secondary. The primary imagination I hold to be the living power and prime agent of all human perception, and as a repetition in the finite mind in the eternal act of creation in the infinite I Am. The secondary imagination I consider as an echo of the former, coexisting with the conscious will, yet still as identical with the primary in the kind of its agency, and differing only in degree, and in the mode of its operation. It dissolves, diffuses, dissipates, in order to re-create; or where this process is rendered impossible, yet still at

37 Coleridge, as quoted in Owen Barfield, *What Coleridge Thought* (Middletown, CT: Wesleyan University Press, 1971), p. 239.

38 Coleridge. This poem is quoted in Mary Warnock, p. 77.

39 *Anima Poetae*, Ernest Hartley, ed. Coleridge (London: William Heinenann, 1885, p. 206).

> all events it struggles to idealise and to unify. It is essentially vital, even as all objects (as objects) are essentially fixed and dead.[40]

The primary imagination is reminiscent of Kant's productive imagination. While it is a power which allows human participation in eternal creativity, it still remains bound to unifying and understanding perception, rooted in that which is given. The Secondary imagination, while similar in kind, breaks free from this bondage and 'dissolves, diffuses … in order to recreate.' This superior imagination works in partnership with the conscious will and therefore is not enslaved to objects which are 'essentially fixed, dead.' Here the imagination is no longer passive but an active combining power creative and recreative of ideas, evocative and provocative of emotion. In Appendix B of *The Statesman's Manual* Coleridge writes:

> Imagination is that reconciling and mediating power which, incorporating the Reason in the Images of Sense, and organising, as it were, the flux of the senses by the permanence and self-circling energies of the reason, gives birth to a system of symbols, harmonious in themselves and consubstantial with the truths of which they are conductors.[41]

This description of the poetic imagination moves our understanding of this faculty beyond its function as image maker to a new appreciation of its creative role in the symbolic construction of language. This link between imagination and language has been elaborated by philosophers in our own century especially in the works of Paul Ricoeur, however it was the Romantic poets who first intimated this understanding. For Coleridge, it is the secondary imagination which creates the tensive balance of metaphoric language, and allows the birth of poetic thought.

Coleridge's understanding of imagination, especially in the Biographia, as that which 'forms into one' offered the possibility of moving beyond the classic dualisms between mind and matter, body and soul. His theoretical position, if taken to its logical conclusion, could have offered a new paradigm for a relational understanding of reality beyond the dichotomies

40 Samuel Taylor Coleridge, *Biographia Literaria*, ed. J. Shawcross, 2 Vols. (Oxford: Oxford University Press, 1907), Vol. I, p. 202.

41 Coleridge, *Statesman's Manual*, ed. R. J. White, p. 28.

prevalent since Plato. However, after finishing the *Biographia* he became fearful of the trajectory of his own thought, especially its propensity towards pantheism. For this reason he distanced himself from his work on imagination from 1818 and for the latter part of his life seldom mentioned the word.[42] Again, the fear of substantial paradigm change effected the suppression of the imagination's radically creative character.

Sadly, Coleridge sought to distance himself from his own insight on imagination towards the end of his life and conceded his failure to pursue his thought to its creative conclusion. Yet it must be stated that both he and the other romantic poets of the nineteenth century moved the imagination from the wings of unimportance to centre stage; from being viewed as a combining faculty (classical), to being a creative facility, or an inner rainbow (romantic). It was now understood as the movement of an arc linking the unconscious and the conscious, memory and meaning, sense and reflection, the empirical and the transcendental, and the cognitive and the affective. Not that imagination replaces any of these activities; rather it is constitutive of them all, binding and weaving and bursting forth in ever new creative beginnings.

This evolution has been the hinge, opening twentieth-century writers in many disciplines to reflect and articulate a new understanding of imagination. No longer is imagination the prerogative of philosophical theory, literature and religious thought. Specialised research in experimental psychology, the anthropological study of symbols and the exploration of fantasy states of mind have expanded ever more positively our understanding of imagination.[43]

While I do not wish to survey each of those new studies, their presence is challenging the formulation of an integrated theory of the imagination. This challenge is taken up most seriously in the works of Paul Ricoeur. Ricoeur now sees his life's work culminating in an articulation of a philosophy of the imagination. He hopes that this philosophy will unveil the

42 For further detail about this period of his life see James Engell, *The Creative Imagination: Enlightenment to Romanticism* (Harvard University Press, 1981), pp. 363ff.

43 For an excellent bibliography in each of these areas see, *American Psychologist* 19 (1964); and *International Philosophical Quarterly* Vol. XVIII, No. 3.

ontological and epistemological significance of the imagination. It is a philosophy that roots itself in the classical/romantic tradition that I have traced, but that flowers in new creative spheres as well.

Ricoeur: The Imagination Constructs Being and Knowing

In this century, Paul Ricoeur has greatly enhanced our appreciation and understanding of imagination. In 1972, he made a unique plea for the development of a philosophy of imagination[44] and his own life and work has been a faithful response to this call.

In his earliest writings, he builds on a Kantian appreciation of imagination and sees it as a faculty with transcendental possibilities. However, Ricoeur soon adds a linguistic dimension to the Kantian understanding. I would claim that Ricoeur's primary contribution is to define the creative imagination as central to all discourse and not simply key in the psychological image-making process:

> Are we not ready to recognise in the power of imagination, no longer the faculty of deriving 'images from our sensory experience', but the capacity for letting new worlds shape our understanding of ourselves?
>
> This power would not be conveyed by images, but by the emergent meanings in our language. Imagination would thus be treated as a dimension of language.[45]

Imagination therefore is not simply the faculty which reproduces images from faded perceptions, nor is it limited to the transcendent epistemological acts highlighted by Kant. It is also a fulcrum in the creation of living language.

44 Paul Ricoeur, 'Creativity in Language', trans. David Pellauer, 17 *Philosophy Today* (Summer, 1973), p. 109.

45 Paul Ricoeur, *Hermeneutics and the Human Sciences. Essays on Language, Actions and Interpretation*, trans. and ed. by J. B. Thompson (Cambridge: Cambridge University Press, 1981), p. 181.

In his work. *The Rule of Metaphor*, Ricoeur develops his claim that language is central to the human aspiration for growth and transformation.[46] Within this project the metaphoric function of language is primary. Ricoeur claims that it is metaphor that impels human discourse towards new meaning and that imagination lies at the heart of the metaphoric process. This is what Ricoeur refers to as the 'semantic role of the imagination.'[47]

In his treatment of metaphor, Ricoeur recalls the Greek root of the word – metapherein – which indicates change or movement. To 'metaphorise' means to carry a term beyond the place where it belongs and thus link it with a context otherwise alien to it. Therefore, he pushes beyond any understanding of metaphor as simply a decorative device in rhetoric discourse. Rather, metaphor is at the heart of discourse; indeed it is its central feature.

The movement towards change initiated by the metaphoric process comprises a moment of deviation, a semantic clash followed by the emergence of new meaning. At the moment of dissonance, the 'meaning-making' imagination holds the differences until a new similarity or commonality can be imaged. Here the productive imagination schematises new meaning without dissolving the differences but doing so through the difference.

> Imagination, accordingly, is this ability to produce new kinds of assimilation and to produce them not above the differences, as in the concept, but in spite of and through the differences. Imagination, within metaphoric discourse, can live easily with difference, feels no need to merge dissimilitude or cast difference in dualistic opposites.[48]

This living with the strange, with the contradiction, can allow truth to be revealed in unexpected ways. This emergence of new meaning pushes open our consciousness to new ways of understanding and of being in the world.

46 Paul Ricoeur, *The Rule of Metaphor: Multi-disciplinary Studies of the Creation of Meaning in Language* (London: Routledge & Kegan Paul, 1978).

47 Paul Ricoeur, 'The Metaphorical Process', in *On Metaphor*, edited by Sheldon Sacks. (Chicago: The University of Chicago Press, 1978).

48 Paul Ricoeur, 'The Metaphorical Process as Cognition, Imagination and Feeling', *Critical Inquiry* (1978–1979), p. 148.

> This schematisation makes the imagination the place for the emergence of the figurative sense in the interplay of identity and difference. And the metaphor is the place in the discourse where this schematisation is visible, because identity and difference are not merged one into the other but opposed.[49]

It is important to note that in the metaphoric movement towards new meaning, imagination fulfils a linguistic as well as an image-making function.[50] In the movement of metaphor, it is the imagination which holds together the 'is' and the 'is not' in tensive balance. The enabler of living metaphor is 'the non-verbal kernel of imagination.'[51] In holding this tension in harmony until new meaning emerges, imagination acts in both a mediatory but also in a creative and independent role. To bring life back to language, to empower words to renew the world is to create and generate living metaphors. It is the productive imagination which sparks the insight, allows 'the seeing' of what otherwise would remain remote. [52]

The Challenge to Religious Discourse

As well as opening up new insight into our ways of understanding the world, living metaphor also shifts our notion of truth. Conceptual language, in its fixity of formulation frequently makes arrogant claims for the absolute or universal nature of its formulations. Metaphoric language, suspended in the creative space between the 'is' and the 'is not' of any claim, restores a modesty and humility to human discourse. This treatment of language allows us to see it as a living organism which needs constantly to be renewed, revitalised, if it is to continue to carry meaning. If, as Ricoeur claims, new metaphors are 'constantly degenerating into

49 Paul Ricoeur, *La Metaphor Vive*, p. 386, translation mine.

50 For further detail on the 'steps' of the metaphoric process see Leonard Lawlor, *Imagination and Chance, The Difference Between the Thought of Ricoeur and Derrida* (New York: State University of New York Press, 1992), pp. 66–70.

51 P. Ricoeur, *The Rule of Metaphor*, p. 199.

52 For further explanation of the productive character of imagination see Paul Ricoeur, 'On Interpretation' in Alan Montefiore (ed.) *Philosophy in France Today* (Cambridge University Press, 1983), p. 184.

stale, dead metaphors',[53] then the challenge to be creative, imaginative, in our use of language is imperative if the words we speak are to hold any meaning, and if we are even to 'lisp the truth' as Emily Dickinson says so well. Much of the language we are subjected to, especially in public religious discourse is but the 'fossilised remains' of what was once living creative metaphor. Language moves through a constant cycle of regeneration – dying and coming to birth – and it is metaphor which is the life force of this renewal. This Ricoeur claims is his 'most extreme hypothesis: namely that the "metaphorical" which transgresses the categorical order also begets it'.[54] Ricoeur unpacks the meaning of this proposal: 'In other words, the power of metaphor would be to break old categorisation, in order to establish new logical frontiers on the ruins of their forerunners.'[55] Metaphoric discourse is that which breaks through the sedimentation, the fossilisation of dead words allowing newness to be envisaged. It is true, as Ricoeur reminds us, that 'one always needs the word to assume the world into a manifestation of the sacred (hierophany)'.[56] However, the word that can unveil the sacred, that can reveal the divine must be a living metaphor freed from the shackles of 'old categorisations' and over familiar conceptualisations.

The Intersection of Metaphor and Imagination

Metaphorical language constantly opens up new meaning, new insights into ways of being and understanding. Imagination is the womb from which metaphors are born. Furthermore, imagination holds the 'tensive balance' so that the meaning of metaphor can be grasped but then metaphor also jolts the imagination into imagining the world in entirely new

53 Gary Madison, *The Hermeneutics of Postmodernity: Figures and Themes* (Bloomington: Indiana University Press, 1990), p. 148.

54 MV, p. 34; Rm 24.

55 MV 151; RM 197-98.

56 Paul Ricoeur, *Freud and Philosophy: An Essay on Interpretation* (New Haven, CT: Yale University Press, 1970); *De L 'interpretain essai sure Freur* (Paris: Edition du Seuil, 1965), p. 124.

ways. This interconnection between metaphor and imagination is at the heart of the renewal of language. What Ricoeur is telling us is that language could be the most creative thing we possess to radically change and transform the world. However, for this to happen we must put life back into language and imagination is the rising agent. At the beginning of an interview with Richard Kearney, Ricoeur stated:

> In *LaMetaphore Vive* [The Rule of Metaphor] I tried to show how language could extend itself to its very limits forever discovering new resonances within itself. The term Vive [living] in the title of this work is all important, for it was my purpose to demonstrate that there is not just an epistemological and political imagination, but also and perhaps more fundamentally a linguistic imagination which generates meaning through the living power of metaphoricity.[57]

Linguistic renewal, rooted in the intersection of metaphor and imagination, undoubtedly opens up new worlds which in turn shape and reshape our understanding of ourselves.[58] However, it must be made clear that Ricoeur's project does not rest simply with claims about epistemological transformation. In opening up new meaning, living metaphor also opens up 'new ways of being in the world'.[59] Towards the end of *The Rule of Metaphor*, Ricoeur spells out the link between metaphor and our ontological vocation. The metaphoric imagination influences not only how we know reality but our very being in the world.

> The semantic aim of metaphorical utterance does intersect most decisively with the aim of ontological discourse … at the point where the reference of metaphorical utterances brings being as actuality and as potentiality into play.[60]

57 Richard Kearney, *Dialogues with Contemporary Thinkers* (Manchester: Manchester University Press, 1984), p. 67

58 A similar point is made by Richard Kearney at the beginning of his excellent chapter on Paul Ricoeur in *Poetics of Imagining: From Husserl to Lyotard* (HarperCollins Academic, 1991), p. 134.

59 Paul Ricoeur, 'Myth as the Bearer of Possible Worlds', in Richard Kearney, ed. *Dialogues with Contemporary Continental Thinkers*.

60 Paul Ricoeur, *The Rule of Metaphor*, p. 307.

Metaphoric imagination pushes open the windows of our understanding and enables us to glimpse new ways of interpreting what has become familiar. But at an even more primordial level, the metaphoric imagination causes us to re-examine the very foundation upon which our lives are structured. New intimations of being are possible if we can sustain the tension at the core of all reality and cultivate the capacity always to image something more. New ways of being emerge from new ways of knowing. New ways of knowing are possible through the creative imagination. As Ricoeur says, 'it is in imagination that the new being is first formed in me'.[61] This challenge to remain open to growth at the deepest level of being and becoming is possible where life is lived in connection to the metaphoric imagination. To touch into the power of imagination is to allow oneself to 'be grasped by new possibilities' where a new world order could open up, involving a redescription of reality.

Many may ask where can we see the type of living language of which Ricoeur speaks; a language which could reorder our way of knowing and being in the world? The answer I propose is in the words of poetry and prophecy. On poetry, Ricoeur quotes Bachelard's well-known statement: 'A poetic image, by its novelty sets in motion the entire linguistic mechanism. The poetic image places us at the origin of the speaking world.'[62] In poetry, truth erupts, unveiling that which otherwise remains cloaked and often choked. Ricoeur argues, 'It is in this sense of manifestation that language in its poetic function is a vehicle of revelation.'[63] And as the Irish poet Derek Mahon reminds us, the hidden source of poetry is 'the watchful heart'[64] – the capacity to live in intimate relation with all reality, including language. But again the manifestation of poetic truth and our response are dependent on imagination. If truth is freed in poetry, it is challenged to root itself in

61 Paul Ricoeur, 'Philosophical Hermeneutics and Theological Hermeneutics', *Studies in Religion* No. 5 (1975–1976), p. 33.

62 G. Bachelard, *Poetics of Space*, trans Maria Mas (Boston, MA: Beacon Press, 1964), x pxis as quoted by R. Kearney in *Poetics of Imagining*, p. 140.

63 P. Ricoeur, 'Towards a Hermeneutic of the Idea of Revelation', *Harvard Theological Review* Vol. 70, 1977, p. 24.

64 Derek Mahon, 'Everything is Going to Be All Right', 1979 *Selected Poems* (Viking/Gallery, 1991).

history by prophecy. The prophetic word activates the historical imagination and calls for transformative action.

Although Ricoeur links discourse and action, I would join with those who claim that in his writings action is subordinate to discourse rather than 'nonreducible twin halves of an undivided history'.[65] In the 1950s, Ricoeur is 'led to seek the cross-roads of need and willing in imagination – imagination of the missing thing and action aimed towards the thing'.[66] His later works demonstrate little evidence as to how the social or political imagination moves us from a position of theoretical reflection to concrete action. How does the redescription of reality lead to the restructuring of reality? This is a key question within a feminist analysis of the imagination. It must be answered if the true nature of the imagination's radical creativity is to be unravelled. I will return to this in the next chapter.

The Male Imagination

This philosophical history of imagination, whether read forward from Plato to the twentieth century or backwards from Ricoeur to the classical Greek period, is a male history and the very understanding of imagination is profoundly influenced by the patriarchal culture in which it is cast. Although we can indicate a trajectory of progress in the appreciation of imagination through the centuries, it is clear there is no gender analysis of this faculty, no mention of a female imagination. The presumption is that imagination is one, part of the 'economy of the same', always to be judged by male hegemony. Further, as I have indicated throughout, the suppression of the imagination – sometimes blatant as in the case of Plato, but most times subtle – sprang from the suspicion that this faculty resembles 'feminine' attributes and therefore must be controlled. Emotion,

65 Calvin O. Schrag, *Communicative Praxis and the Space of Subjectivity* (Bloomington: Indiana University Press, 1986), pp. 170–171.

66 Paul Ricoeur, *Freedom & Nature: The Voluntary and the Involuntary* (Northwestern, 1966), p. 96.

materiality, passion, creativity and action belong to a world other than reason, pure form, objectivity and interpretative discourse. Though the male philosophers often came to the edge of seeing and affirming this other world, they always held back.

My proposal is this: to genuinely free the imagination to its rightful place, to allow it to become the faculty which is central to both our being and knowing, as Ricoeur proposes, it is vital that we recognise the existence of and the difference between the female and male imagination. The theorist I have found most helpful in this task is the French philosopher and psychoanalyst Luce Irigaray.

The Female Imaginaire: Luce Irigaray

Although Irigaray has not developed a systematic philosophy of the imagination, the creativity of her writings opens up a clearing in the imagination which allows us to understand the female dimension of this central function of human life. The primary aim of Irigaray's work, as I have mentioned earlier, is to inaugurate an acceptance, an appreciation of sexual difference. However, at the heart of this project lies the imagination. We live in a world where the maleness, the sameness of patriarchal societies has shaped the social signification, representation of all reality. Put otherwise, our world is a construct of the 'male imaginaire.' If we want a world beyond patriarchy, a world of mutuality, then we must give expression to the 'female imaginaire', must allow female images and metaphors of a new world order to find a public voice.

The word 'imaginaire' is not directly translatable into English and is used in a variety of ways in Irigaray's writing. In her early work *Speculum of the Other Woman*,[67] the concept has a psychoanalytic reference, rooted above all in her critique of Freud and Lacan. However, 'the imaginary emerges from its relatively subordinate position in *Speculum* to become in

67 Luce Irigary, *Speculum of the Other Woman*, trans by Gillian c. Gill (Ithaca: Cornell University Press, 1985).

"This Sex Which is Not One" and "An Ethics of Sexual Difference", one of the key notions of an ambitious social critique'.[68]

The search for the female imaginaire is a process which calls firstly for the dissolution, the dismembering by critique, of the universal, neutral male imaginaire which underpins Western metaphysics. This dissolution entails exposing how the patriarchal imagination has relegated 'the feminine' to its unconscious, imagining woman as 'the other of the same', the negative aspects of maleness.[69] Irigaray demonstrates that this 'conscious phantasy' is a nothingness; it is an illusion that has little to do with real women. Secondly, she argues that far from being neutral, the male imaginaire is sexual and rooted in male bodiliness. The oneness and the fixity of the patriarchal order is a symbolic representation of the phallus which dominates the male imaginaire. Irigaray challenges the male philosophers: 'The symbolic that you impose as a universal, free of all empirical or historical contingency, is your imaginary transformed into an order, a social order.'[70]

However, Irigaray is not simply interested in a critique of the phallocratic order, her interest, especially in her recent work, is to reconstruct, to bring to birth, to nourish, to mentor a female imaginaire.[71] The female imaginaire is rooted in a retrieval of women's bodiliness. By accepting and

68 Margaret Whitford, *Luce Irigaray: Philosophy in the Feminine* (London: Routledge, 1991), p. 66. One of the many contributions of Margaret Whitford's work on Luce Irigaray is her emphasis that the imaginaire has a 'projective dimension'. One should 'conceive of the creation of the female imaginary as a social process involving intervention in the symbolic' (p. 90). This interconnection between imagination and language is something we have encountered in the writings of Paul Ricoeur and it is vital for a correct understanding of Luce Irigaray. In so exposing the social, political dimension of her exposition of a female imaginaire one answers those critics who dismiss her work as essentialist or naturalist.

69 'We shall die together if you do not let me go outside your sameness' Luce Irigaray *Elemental Passions* Translated by Joanne Collie & Judity Still (London: The Athlone Press, 1992), p. 14.

70 Luce Irigaray, Parler n 'est jamais neutre (Paris: Minuit, 1985), p. 269, as quoted by Margaret Whitford, *Luce Irigaray: Philosophy in the Feminine*, p. 90.

71 According to Whitford, Irigaray posits three different senses in her understanding of the female imaginary. 'There is the position of the female in the male imaginary; there are the scraps or debris of what might be an alternative imaginary (a fragmented female imaginary); and there is the anticipation of a more fully deployed

reflecting on female sexuality as unique and by giving voice to the imagery which emerges from this reflection, women can bring to public voice and ultimately shape the symbolic order by the statement of our own specificity. In her own creative fashion, Irigaray has demonstrated in her writings the concreteness and the political power inherent in this faculty.

The task is multiple. Firstly, Irigaray challenges women to symbolise, to bring to public voice from their own unique perception, the various relationships of their lives. This move from being described and thus controlled, to describing from outside the male imaginaire will allow women to reclaim their being. Language will be 'recovered, reinvented' as 'women speaking among women' deliberately seek to shape the symbolic order.[72]

In a passage demonstrating a female poetics, Irigaray clearly leaves male modes of expression as she speaks of female lovers: 'Erection is no business of ours: we are at home on flatlands.'[73] For Irigaray, self-love, love for other women, connectedness between women is needed for the birth of a 'female sexuality … a female imaginaire … a female language.'[74] As mentioned, the mother-daughter relationship must also be symbolised. This will be a further expression of the female imagination and will affect the public image of women in our society today.

> There was a time, Irigaray reminds us, when mother and daughter were the figure of a natural and social model. It was a time of harmony among and between the sexes. This couple was the guardian of the fertility of nature in general and of the relations to the divine. This time existed and corresponds to centuries of history known today as prehistory.[75]

The mother must celebrate her maternal creative capacity but must also refuse any attempt to reduce her to this role. In a patriarchal imaginaire 'femininity fades away before maternity, is absorbed into maternity. The

---

female imaginary which might exist in creative intercourse with the male.' See Philosophy in the Feminine, pp. 67–68.

72 Luce Irigaray, *This Sex Which is Not One*, Trans, by Catherine Porter (Cornell University Press, 1985, p. 119).

73 Ibid., p. 213.

74 Ibid., p. 33.

75 SP, 206. As quoted by Whitford, Philosophy in the Feminine, p. 177.

mother once again ... mask(s) the woman.'[76] In the collapse of femaleness into motherhood, women are robbed of their identities as woman, as sexual beings, and daughters are deprived of the image of a strong woman who is their mother. There is therefore a personal and political reason for 'recognising your mother as a woman ... distancing yourself from motherly omnipotence. You recognise her as a finite person with limits ...'[77]

The other side of this inauguration of the matemal/woman from the perspective of the female imaginaire is the recognition that we are always mothers once we are women. Again Irigaray reminds us: 'We bring something other than children into the world, we engender something other than children: love, desire, language, art, the social, the political, the religious for example. But this creation has been forbidden us for centuries, and we must reappropriate this maternal dimension that belongs to us as women.'[78] The challenge to women is to claim time and space to touch our own uniqueness, our own creativity, and then, without apology or permission, bring it to public expression.

The restructuring of relationship from a perspective that includes a female as well as a male imagination would include a whole other understanding of heterosexual relationship. In her book, *An Ethics of Sexual Difference*, Irigaray states: 'If the one of love is ever to be achieved, we have to discover the two.' Women must speak 'of her own jouissance, her sexuate body, "her own desire" as she enters such a relationship'.

> A genesis of love between the sexes has yet to come about in all dimensions, from the smallest to the greatest, from the most intimate to the most political. A world that must be created or recreated so that man and woman may once again or at last live together, meet and sometimes inhabit the same place.[79]

76 *Speculum*, pp. 74, 117. See also *Speculum* 234.

77 Kiki Amsberg & Aafke Steentiuis, "An Interview with Luce Irigaray," trans. Robert van Krieken, *Hecate* 9 (1983): 198, 195.

78 Luce Irigaray, "The bodily encounter with the mother," p. 43 as cited in the *Irigaray Reader*, ed. by Margaret Whitford (London: Basil Blackwell, 1991).

79 *Ethics*, p. 17.

As women give voice to their imaginaire, stating what relationship would look like in a new order, an order of mutuality, Irigaray makes it quite clear that she has no desire simply 'to reverse the order of things. Even supposing this to be possible, history would repeat itself in the long run, would revert to sameness: to phallocratism. It would leave room neither for women's sexuality, nor for women's imaginary, nor for women's language to take (their) place'.[80] With an aspiration for a social order of mutual sustainment, women must courageously voice their imagery in new symbolic expression so as to expose the lie of the exclusivist male imaginaire with all its fantasies and distortions of the 'feminine'. Irigaray encourages women to give expression to this new order using metaphors rooted in female bodiliness, metaphors which startle awareness of woman as a sexual, sensual being in her own right.

The call to a female poetics as a means of expressing the female imaginaire, also demands a critique of male metaphoric thought. Ricoeur has correctly indicated that living metaphor is the basis of all language. The stultification of language, its fall to meaninglessness, leaves in its wake faded and jaded metaphors which have had their day. What Ricoeur does not highlight is that within a closed patriarchal order, even the most creative metaphoric construction lacks its transformative potential, as it is conceived in and remains bound to an exclusivist world order. In other words, the overriding metaphor of patriarchy is sameness thus, in the end, blocking difference, which is the seed of creativity. As Irigaray sees it, women have been stifled beneath all those eulogistic or denigratory metaphors of patriarchal discourse, they have been 'rolled up in metaphors' which have bound and gagged them.[81]

In the construction of a female poetics, Irigaray prefers metonymic as opposed to a metpahoric discourse. If, as we have seen, metaphor gives birth to newness in the disruption of the old, the familiar, metonymic creative expression erupts in contiguity and connection with the old. She looks for originality in new combinations rather than in disruption. The new, though never identical, is neighbour of the old.

80 TS, p. 33.

81 Irigaray, *Speculum of the Other Woman*, p. 143.

Her metonymic discourse is rooted in female bodiliness, female sexuality. Her use of images of the body such as 'the two lips' are profoundly evocative and deeply ambiguous. Which lips is she speaking of you ask? The answer is both, in multivarious combinations – discursive lips touching and formulating new symbolic worlds – genital lips 'in continuous contact',[82] namely, 'the contact of at least two (lips) which keeps woman in touch with herself, but without any possibility of distinguishing what is touch from what is touched'.[83] Irigaray goes on to state: 'Far from being essentialist or literalist, such language both subverts and heals the exclusivist male imaginaire which phantasies and objectifies female sexuality. Furthermore, such imagery is giving a "woman to woman language"; a language which will in time combat other prevailing discourses.'[84]

Irigaray further critiques the 'patriarchal imagination' for its false presentation of another aspect of female corporeality, namely the placenta. Contrary to male projections of fusion, the placenta has 'relative autonomy' and plays 'a mediating role during intrauterine life'. The placenta 'establishes a relationship between mother and foetus' nurturing and sustaining each without collapsing one into the other. A female imaginaire reflecting such bodily imagery into the world of symbolic discourse challenges once again the notion of sameness and promotes the distinction, the otherness, the difference that promotes life.[85]

Such imagery born in a female imaginaire breaks the silence about women's sexuality as viewed by women. Irigaray's boldness, in making explicit what has been hushed or ignored by patriarchy, gives women permission to give expression to their bodiliness in a manner which must

82 Irigarav, TS:24.

83 Irigaray, TS:26.

84 E. Groz, *Irigaray and the Divine*, as quoted by Margaret Whitford in 'Irigaray's Body Symbolic', Hypatia Vol. 6, No. 3 (Fall 1991), p. 100.

85 Luce Irigaray, *Je, tu, nous: Towards a Culture of Difference*, Chapter 4, On the Maternal Order: A Dialogue between Luce Irigaray and Helene Rouch, trans. by Alison Martin (London: Routledge, 1993), pp. 37–44. Another aspect of female corporeality imaged in Irigaray's work is 'the mucous'. For example, see *Sexes and Genealogies*, trans. by Gillian Gill (New York: Columbia University Press, 1993). For an excellent analysis of this image in Irigaray's work see Margaret Whitford, 'Irigaray's Body Symbolic', especially pp. 101–103.

ultimately shift and shape a new symbolic order. Poet Ntozake Shange speaks of this challenge in another context:

> My work attempts to ferret out what I know and touch in a woman's body ....
>
> I discuss the simple reality of going home at nite, of washing one's body, looking out the window with a woman's eyes, we must learn our common symbols, preen them and share them with the world.[86]

The expression of a new poetics of woman's subjectivity, rooted in a female imaginary, will be enhanced by reclaiming elemental language. To speak of our experience using the living metaphors of earth, air, fire and water, allows us to return to the stuff from which we are made and which continues to sustain us. In *Divine Woman* Irigaray tells us that in her writing she:

> was anxious to go back to those natural matters that constitute the origin of our bodies, of our life, of our environment, the flesh of our passion ... We still pass our daily lives in a universe that is composed and is known to be composed of four elements: air, water, fire and earth. We are made up of these elements and we live in them. They determine, more or less freely, our attractions, our affects, our passions, our limits, our aspirations.[87]

To reclaim the rich resources of elemental language will enable women to circumvent the usual depictions of their existence from within the patriarchal imaginary. Mined and explored by the female imagination, the four elements could provide a new foundation for women to express a poetics of the corporeality and passion of their existence. Such language would open understanding and encourage the expression of the materiality of our origins, the earthedness of our present existence and the interconnectedness of all reality. Such language would bring us back to our senses and give us a new awareness of the simplicity and the mystery of the core of life.

In calling us to root our imaginations in the elements and out of this to return to the cosmic to allow a new language to emerge, Irigaray is calling

86 Shange, *For Colored Girls Who Have Considered Suicide When the Rainbow Is Enuf* (New York: Bantam Books, 1981), p. 1.

87 Irigaray, *Sexes and Genealogies*, p. 157.

us to go back to our origins and to a time before history in which, as I indicated at the beginning of this chapter, God was a woman and women were at home on earth. She writes: 'It seems to me that we certainly have to incite a return to the cosmic, but at the same time asking ourselves why we were stopped as we were becoming divine.'[88] The journey back to reinstating a divine transcendent that images and empowers female becoming will be facilitated by elemental language. Such imagery from the past will give new confidence to the present struggle to establish structures that both reflect and enable the full potential of female and male existence.

Once female imaginaire is discovered and given voice, 'the oneness', 'the neutrality' and 'the subjectivity' of the patriarchal imagination will be exposed as simply untrue. Men will thus have the humbler but surely the more creative role of giving expression to their own imagination – lightly owning it as simply that – the male rather than the universal imagination.

Conclusion

Moving towards a feminist imagination of love and the related work of establishing a new world order is, I believe, dependent on the restoration and expression of both the female and male imagination. Imagination, steeped in an understanding of sexual difference, will open up images of the possible and encourage action towards the possible horizon of mutual love. Our hope for a new future lies in an imagination rooted in love. For it is in choosing to love that the rebirth of self and others can be realised. It is living out of a context of powerful love, not powerful dominance, that relationships can be formed which allow the other to be other and not reduced to the same. An imagination informed by love will allow us to mediate between and move beyond the many false dichotomies that have marred the potential of full human becoming.

It is now that we are in a better position to repossess the secret of love. It is now that we may fruitfully move towards images and actions of love.

88 *Ibid*, p. 60.

CHAPTER FIVE

Dreaming Love

> We have thought too much in terms of a will which submits and not enough in terms of an imagination which opens up.[1]
>
> – Paul Ricoeur

Throughout this book I have shown how feminism must embrace the imagination so that the critique and challenges of this framework can shape a new world. The promise and prophecy of a feminist imagination remain unfulfilled, though, until it is historically realised, practically concretised.

We have seen that a new imaginative understanding of women – women's subjectivities and women's identities – requires a corresponding programme of action. Indeed, I would hold that it is only in the context of political action that the new feminist subject, the new way of perceiving reality, can be developed. We have also examined the importance of language in shaping the understanding of who we are and who we might become. Generating imaginative language is, as I have indicated, foundational to imagining human flourishing. Radical change in ways of being and becoming will only be conceived by an imaginative revolution in discourse. Yet, as I discussed in the last chapter, a revolution in discourse must be complemented by a restructuring of reality. While imaging and speaking new language out of the female and male imagination is foundational action for a new world, it must be complemented by diverse social activity to create concretely that new world. Otherwise, the radical discourse will be co-opted by the people and systems that structure personal and social power in dominating rather than loving ways.

1 Paul Ricoeur, 'Hermeneutique de fidee de Revelation', as quoted by R. Kearney in *Poetics of Imagining*, p. 139.

We also saw that a central component of the revolution in discourse is a critical evaluation of our imaginatively constructed understanding of divinity. In light of a feminist critique, the traditional concepts and images have become 'intuitively implausible'.[2] However, an essential dimension of creating new discourse for the Sacred requires us to answer the question: how does this naming inspire ethical action? Finally, we analysed the nature and character of the imagination itself. In fashioning the features of a feminist imagination, I concluded that our hope for a new future lies in an imagination rooted in love. Only in this way, I believe, will a feminist imagination impel us towards ethical activities that create a culture of love, and social structures which foster a love of difference. Let us now consider some of the ingredients that enable us to dream and act towards such love.

Foundational Concerns for the Feminist Ethical Imagination

A Community of Love: The Context for Ethical Imaginings

In this post-modern age, when deconstruction and fragmentation are all about us, there is a growing unease and uncertainty. As age-old truths are dismissed as baggage from a bygone era there is a need – more than ever before – for an imagination that can sustain hope, that can posit an ethical challenge, and that can inspire radical commitment to the works of justice and mutual sustainment. I am suggesting that this ethical imagination must be rooted in and sustained by a community of love and friendship, a community of solidarity amidst differences. The empowerment to live and act radically can best be resourced from within such a context. To mount an imaginative resistance against the techno-economic-social paradigm which shapes twenty-first-century living calls initially for the formation of prophetic communities of love.

2 Gordon Kaufmann, 'Metaphysics and Theology', in *The Theological Imagination: Constructing the Concept of God* (Philadelphia: Westminster Press: 1981), p. 261.

Such communities sustain and hold imaginative actions for transformation; they also inspire and encourage further action. There is no doubt in my mind that individual potential to live and act imaginatively is far greater when we stand in solidarity amidst difference than when we act alone. Katherine Zappone puts it well:

> Acknowledging and incorporating difference is far more than a theoretical adventure ... Its value does not lie in the theoretical realm only. The praxis of living with difference, namely, stepping outside the racial, sexual, cultural and/or class separations that we inherit, provides a grace-filled path to know, respect and love the difference.
>
> Above all it teaches me how to cope creatively with the inherent conflicts of difference rather than ignore or obliterate them. In this I discover the meaning of 'solidarity' and its significance for political change that will benefit myself and women who are not like me at all.[3]

There is here an ethical summons to women to create communities of love – not exclusive of men – but intolerant of sexism and any injustice, especially poverty, that reduces women's potential and does not accept her difference. We can say that few such communities exist, which is understandable, as they depend on women imaging a self and world that by and large is not yet realised. However, the horizon of this world is brought closer every time we act imaginatively and reflect critically from within such a feminist community context. For such a context raises the level of critical consciousness and through various creative processes allows new patterns of living to become accessible, new models of participation to become visible.

Having co-founded such a community some years ago, I am now more convinced than ever that the translation of imaginative dreams to reality is commensurate with the love and the creativity of the community which forms to enact it. The Shanty Educational Project was founded to offer women in very disadvantaged areas educational and enterprise opportunities. Today, ten years on, I am convinced that the success of this project is rooted in the community of women, who come from a rich diversity of

3 Katherine Zappone, 'Woman's Special Nature': A Different Horizon for Theological Anthropology', *Concilium* 1991, p. 93.

backgrounds, who partner together with extraordinary commitment and friendship to achieve a common goal, a goal which is ever changing and ever new. I agree with Sharon Welch when she states:

> An appropriate symbol for the process of celebrating life, enduring limits and resisting injustice is not the Kingdom of God, it is the beloved community … The 'beloved community' names the matrix within which life is celebrated, love is worshipped, and partial victories over injustice lay the groundwork for further acts of criticism and courageous defiance.[4]

To this symbolic naming of 'the beloved community' as the place and context for transformative action I would add the word 'feminist'. A feminist community will not simply resist and critique all manner of gender oppression but will act creatively to shape a new world of mutual relations across the differences.

Imaging the Possible

From within the context of a loving and creative community, the imagination pushes and the boundaries expand into an abundance of possibility, captured powerfully in Adrienne Rich's *Phantasia, for Elvira Statayeu*, where she celebrates the women mountaineers who had the courage to imagine the possible. [5]

As Emily Dickinson reminds us, 'possibility is the fuse lit by the spark of imagination.' It is the imagination which allows the 'perhaps' to blossom, the 'possible' to become reality. It is this sense of possibility that gives us the will to change, to know that things and people could be otherwise.[6] Husserl states that, 'in the realm of imagination's arbitrary freedom we can lift all actuality to a plane of pure possibility'.[7] Further, I am convinced that

4 *A Feminist Ethic of Risk*, pp. 160–161.

5 *The Fact of a Doorframe: Poems Selected and New 1950–1984* (New York: W.W. Norton & Company, 1984) p. 226–227.

6 Similar point made by Richard Kearney in *Poetics of Imagining*, p. 216.

7 As quoted by Edward S. Casey in *Imagining: A Phenomenological Study* (Bloomington: Indiana University Press, 1979), p. 199.

there need be no discrepancy between an image of what ought to be and its realisation in the creation of the new.

Imagination can also allow us to see the possibility for newness in the everydayness of our lives. It allows us to break from the jaded patterns of humdrum existence and risk living for the impossible. As Mary Warnock suggests: 'We can use imagination to render our experience unfamiliar and mysterious.'[8] Pushing the boundaries of the familiar, prising open the present to reveal a new future is part of the redemptive work of the imagination. It is a work that we should embrace consciously and deliberately in the realisation that we become what we image. As Eavan Boland states: 'An object of the images we make is what we are …'[9]

The necessary ingredient, as I have said before, is that such images, such aspirations, are seeded within a community whose love will bring them to fruition. It is within such a community that images of the possible can undergo a 'dramatic rehearsal' (Dewey) before being concretised in political action.

Imaging Utopia

Paul Ricoeur reminds us that the horizon of the possible is expanded and enlarged by the imagination's capacity to create utopias. In an article titled 'Imagination in Discourse and Action', Ricoeur develops his understanding of the social imagination: 'The touchstone of the practical function of the imagination.'[10] He speaks about the 'free play of possibility' which the social imagination opens up, especially its capacity to image, to vision utopias.

The word 'utopia' means 'no where', coined by Thomas More for his work of that name in 1516; it comes from the Greek *Ou-topia*. This land without place gives us another vantage point from which to image the

8 D. Sloan, *Insight-Imagination The Emancipation of Thought and the Modem World* (Connecticut: Greenwood Press, 1983), p. 147.

9 'The Art of Grief' *In a Time of Violence* (Carcenet Press, 1994), p. 52.

10 Ricoeur, 'Imagination in Discourse and Action', in *Analecta Husserliana: Yearbook of Phenomenological Research*, Vol. 7, 1978, p. 3.

possible. Standing imaginatively in this nonspace we can 'radically rethink' what we have come to accept as reality. From this distance – looking back – we realise with new clarity that what we have accepted as given is simply socially constructed reality and can change. A Utopian stance can be highly subversive, it can 'unmask the pretensions inherent in all systems of legitimation'[11] and can give us new insight into the 'paradoxes of power' that dominate our world. Furthermore, the capacity to stand 'no where' looking back can give new freedom to imagination's critical capacity. Standing in this 'other' space gazing backwards allows the bland sameness of present reality to come into sharp relief.

The Utopian placelessness not only affords an oasis from which to critique the present and the past, it above all allows the creative imaginative context from which to construct what could be. While outside space, a utopian vision stands in time. The political vision from 'no where' challenges us 'now here' to realise, to concretise this imaginary place.[12] There are, as Ricoeur cautions, many kinds of utopian visions; some less helpful than others. From the eighteenth and nineteenth centuries we have inherited a Romantic utopianism which frequently projected a static idealised vision of the future. Such projections are decidedly unhelpful as they are simply amplifications of the present and leave little room for the radical possibility of change and newness which the future can unfurl. If, as I have claimed, we accept that present reality is socially constructed, constantly in flux, in process, then surely the challenge is not to preordain the future in static formulations but to act to create it. Luce Irigaray, supporting this dynamic understanding of utopianism, questions 'a desire to anticipate and codify the future, rather than to work here and now to construct it. To concern oneself in the present about the future certainly does not consist in programming it in advance but in trying to bring it into existence.'[13]

11 Ibid., p. 19.

12 See Irigaray, *Ethics of Sexual Difference*. A similar point is made by Eva T. H. Brann in her new book. *The World of the Imagination: Sun and Substance*. Maryland: Rowman & Littlefield Publisher, Inc. 1991, p. 715.

13 In *Shifting Scenes: Interviews on Women, Writing and Politics in Post '68 France*, eds, Alice Jardine and Anne Menke (New York: Columbia University Press, 1991), p. 41.

Her insistence is on 'struggle' in the present to create a new social order where women could find their place in the symbolic as well as in the natural order.[14] This struggle in the present to create a future that is new, must be continuous and ongoing. Irigaray agrees that Utopian vision is helpful as it allows us 'to imagine the unimaginable'[15]; it can effect a shift in consciousness and allow us to alter present direction so as to arrive at a different future, above all a future that acknowledges women's difference.

Feminist authors such as Ursula le Guin and Marge Piercy have written some of their finest work in this genre of 'dynamic utopia'. In *Always Coming Home* Le Guin's character Stone Telling narrates her journey from a matrilineal community to a war-centred, death-filled patriarchal society and then finally her 'coming home.'[16] It is a story of passage from life, through death, to 'death's opposite'. The fictional weaving of ancient past with imagined future engenders hope that we as women could realise such a utopia. It is simply a matter of first 'coming home', returning to a past deeply embedded in our memories. From this stance in memory a new confidence is born to engage the process of constructing a future where women count. Telling stories, as these novelists do, creates cultures and expands our horizon of reality. The narration in time of a political vision where mutuality in structure and relationship exist, motivates action towards such a future. Le Guin's writings endow great expectation with the 'authority of the imagination'.[17]

Ricoeur cautions that future imaginings, utopian visions, must remain moored to traditional understandings. Images of 'new worlds' must remain connected to the actual world; the future must link with the present, otherwise it will be cut adrift and rendered meaningless. He speaks of a

14 See Margaret Whitford, *Luce Irigary, Philosophy in the Feminine* (London: Routledge. 1991), see her chapter on 'Feminism and Utopia', pp. 9–25.

15 *Ibid.*, p. 22.

16 (New York: Bantam Books, 1987). Other novels by Ursula Le Guin which are also set in the future and which force us to radically rethink the here and now are: *The Earthsea Trilogy, The Eye of the Heron, Very Far Away from Anywhere Else.*

17 This phrase was used by Ursula Le Guin in her description of Carolyn See's work. *See Dancing At the Edge of the World* (New York: Grove Press, 1989), p. 302.

'dangerously schizophrenic utopian discourse which projects a static fixture without ever producing the conditions for its realisation'.[18]

A feminist imagination sees things quite differently. While aware of the wisdom of weaving future vision into the warp of past and present time, we are equally aware that patriarchal constructions of society cannot anchor feminist fantasy for a new future. Women know intuitively that holding 'utopian expectations' in tandem with patriarchal traditions will bring solutions which are meaningless. As Audre Lorde correctly reminds us: 'The masters' tools will never dismantle the master's house.'[19] To act towards the concretisation of feminist utopian visions calls for a radical break with the traditions and present incarnations of patriarchal reality. But texts such as Le Guin's remind us that an effective archaeology of the past can unearth deep memory and provide a seed-bed for feminist utopias to flower. Furthermore, feminist communities of solidarity amidst difference – existing at the edge of this present world – can be the locus in time for examining and experimenting with the vision from 'no where'.

The counterpoint to Utopia is dystopia and again feminist authors have contributed to this genre. Margaret Atwood's *The Handmaid's Tale* (1985) is a tale of terror forewarning its readers of the kind of future we can expect if the present excesses of patriarchy go unchecked. The depiction of women's exploitation and oppression should jolt us from present complacency and energise action in the present so that we radically alter our direction and navigate towards a very different future.

The Jewish/Christian understanding of 'parousia' somewhat parallels the notion of Utopia. Parousia is a belief that at the 'end-time' a further inbreaking of Divinity will take place in history. This belief has nurtured the ethical imagination of some, giving hope that in the fullness of time evil will be overcome and a cosmic healing will take place. It seems easier to sustain the struggle in the present, however hopeless, if the future vision is of wholeness and completion.

18 Ricoeur, 'Creativity in Language', in *The Philosophy of Paul Ricoeur*, eds C. Regan and D. Stewart (Boston: Beacon, 1973), p. 230.

19 This is the title of an essay in Audre Lorde's collection *Sister Outsider* (New York: The Crossing Press, 1984), p. 110.

However, the bridge between the present and this affirmative future must be to act freely to realise the good. It is, as I have indicated previously, imagination that opens up the vision of the possible in the now, so that a different future can be realised.

Praxis of Imagination

Imaging a different future means little unless these images are acted upon and realised. This is captured beautifully in Audre Lorde's poem 'Starting All Over Again' [20] where she writes about the importance of bringing together our longing and our action. Imagination must 'wither into truth' (Yeats), and must be practically implemented. We must act what we image. Sartre puts it well: 'As people we are nothing other than our project, we exist only insofar as we realise ourselves. Thus we are nothing other than the whole of our actions, nothing more than our lives.'[21] Liberation theologies have taken seriously this call to action, this obligation to root theory in practice. Based in a new imaginative construct, these theologies imply a reformulation of the relationship between religious theory and action. Praxis, which is the interconnection of reflection with action, has been integral to the development of various liberation theologies throughout the globe. Clodovis Boff in his recent book on *Praxis and Theology* states that 'theology of liberation finds its point of departure, its milieu and its finality in praxis. (Praxis) holds primacy over theory, indeed it is the criterion of the verification of theology.'[22] These theologies have as their goal the freedom from oppression of various marginalised peoples. Gustavo Gutierriez, whose work for people living in poverty in Latin America is rightly acclaimed, put it another way: praxis is the first act of 'doing' theology. One's reflection simply follows one's action with and on behalf of the poorest of the poor. The reflection involves a

20 Audre Lorde, 'Starting All Over Again, Jan 1, 1992', in The Marvellous Arithmetics of Distance *Poems 1987–1992* (New York: W.W. Norton & Co. 1993), p. 42.

21 From Maxine Green, *Teacher as Stranger*, p. 282.

22 *Praxis and Theology: Epistemological Foundations* (New York: Maryknoll: Orbis, 1987), p. vxii.

dialogue or a critical correlation between lived experience and the sacred writings of tradition. Rather than being informed of what is 'God's will' for them, the oppressed group give voice themselves to their interpretation of the sacred texts. Thus new meaning is born; divinity is incarnated from the underside of history. New insights and understandings can give those who have been oppressed new courage to resist their plight and act.

Feminist and womanist theologies follow similar methods of liberating praxis. They call for a way of acting and being that is other than what is accepted as commonplace today. They recognise that the new selfhood of women is born in the integration of action and reflection and not simply in knowledge alone.

Imagination remains central to the liberative praxis of feminism. It posits images in anticipation of absent reality; it also motivates by sustaining the will to action through its constant representation of the intended goal in image-making form.[23] It takes us beyond the critical dimension of analysis/theory and impels us to realise the creative images. Furthermore, if, as I have claimed, imagination is not simply an image-making faculty but a way of being, then a feminist imagination challenges us to translate the dream of a world of mutual relations into reality by our actions. Here again, a feminist community can open up creative dialogue which allows us to discern new patterns of living. Images for prophetic action can be tested in the shared wisdom of the community. This context of discernment and dialogue can inspire and hasten the translation of image into action. The imagination of each one will be different and will focus on different projects, but the urgency to act for a world where justice for all is realised, will be similar.

The Ethics of Sexual Difference

Traditionally, the call to action was codified in a clearly delineated set of moral absolutes. Rights, laws and duties were articulated in universal

23 A point made by Paul Ricoeur in *The Philosophy of Paul Ricoeur: An Anthology of His Work* by Charles E. Reagan and David Stewart (Beacon Press, 1978), p. 12.

terms and commanded unquestioning obedience. Formal and abstract thinking was engaged to discern the ethical project. Moral reasoning transcended contextualised experience. The clarity of rules, obligations and moral ideals gave a stability to the ethical response so that one was in little doubt about the right or wrong of any given action. As would be anticipated, this model fails to recognise the foundational role of imagination in ethical reasoning. Yet, as Mark Johnson reminds us, all our reasoning is grounded in the nature of our bodily experience and 'is structured by various kinds of imaginative processes'. Therefore, 'moral understanding depends in large measure on various structures of imagination, such as images, image schemas, metaphors, narratives and so forth.'[24]

The feminist critique of ethics has called into question the clarity and the certainty of the traditional model. Viewed from the perspective of female subjectivity, patriarchal ethics is simply a construct of the male imagination. Universal claims as to the nature of the good and the true, frequently lose their credibility when placed in dialogue with women's understanding of the moral life. It has become clear that we need new models of moral reasoning that encompass the female as well as the male imaginative aspects of understanding. I use the plural 'models' deliberately and agree with Johnson when he reminds us that 'the great diversity of goods that make up the content of our moral experience and present us with real dilemmas cannot be resolved by absolute principles.'[25] In fact, I would claim that the Enlightenment heritage of moral absolutes and universal principles has greatly narrowed the field of ethics and atrophied the moral imagination.

In the 1980s, people like Carol Gilligan, Nel Nodding and Sara Ruddick gave expression to the female moral imagination by counterposing the traditional ethics of justice, of rules and obligation with an ethics of care and responsibility. Listening to the different voices of women, their ethical model is rooted in the concreteness of experience and has a central emphasis on relationality. Moral criteria are drawn up against the backdrop

24 Mark Johnson, *Moral Imagination: Implications of Cognitive Science for Ethics* (Chicago: The University of Chicago Press, 1993), p. ix.

25 *Ibid.*, p. 249.

of life lived in relation, in caring. Ruddick argues: 'Maternal thinking articulates a different perspective on relationships, a perspective expressed independently and therefore confirmed in the morality of love.'[26]

Although each of these authors have been critiqued – Gilligan for her liberalism; Nodding for her rather narrow understanding of care and Ruddick for her over-emphasis on the maternal relationship – their contribution in highlighting the fact that women and men respond with different moral voices cannot be underestimated. Tackling the issue of 'difference' differently than the aforementioned authors, Luce Irigary insists that sexual difference must find its voice and its own ethics. In the reigning ethical imagination men define women. For Irigaray, an ethics of sexual difference would be an ethics that would recognise the subjectivity of each sex, the moral agency of each sex and the need for each sex to shape the public ethical discourse.[27]

The challenge of the 1990s [and the twenty-first century] is to weave a feminist ethical imagination that enables an integration of the various ethical perspectives that have been articulated over the past two decades. Gilligan herself pleads for the integration of the 'male' principle, with the 'female' care-oriented, ethics. Irigaray calls for a 'sensible transcendental' as the condition for an ethics of sexual difference. Weaving this tapestry will not be easy. Holding in harmony what many perceive to be inevitable dichotomies is indeed a task for the imagination. The challenge will be to allow the universal and the particular, the experiential and the rational, the sexual and the spiritual find voice in a variety of ethical models. Such integration must be rooted in an awareness and understanding of sexual difference.

This holding in tandem the universal and the particular is especially important in a post-modem period where respect for difference and diversity can be threatened by a relativism which is destructive and paralysing. A feminist ethics, open to the integration of elements which have been formerly dichotomised, will not hurry towards a new bland generic response

26 Sara Ruddick, 'Remarks on Sexual Politics of Reason', in *Women & Moral Theory*, eds, E. Kittay and D. Meyers (Towota, NJ: Rowman & Littlefield, 1987), p. 352.

27 See L. Irigaray, *Thinking the Difference: For a Peaceful Revolution* (London: The Athlone Press, 1994), see especially the first essay, 'A Chance to Live', pp. 3–35.

to the problems of our age but rather will cull wisdom from a rich variety of different voices. Above all, this requires us to attend to the moral experience of communities of love, resistance and imaginative struggle, of those who live in danger.

For such a mutual integration of perspective to come about, women must recognise and claim their power as moral agents. Traditionally only males could make moral judgements, create moral meaning and values and dictate correct moral choices. The feminist ethical imagination challenges women to step into the public ethical arena as agents empowered to act and to choose the moral good. As moral agents, women must seek to ensure that what has been neglected or ignored in prior formulations of moral principles is now both recognised and celebrated. As agents women must insist that the male bias in ethics is eradicated. Allison Jagger points out this is not an easy task: 'Such bias can be demonstrated only through detailed arguments showing that specific claims or assumptions, evident in specific texts, function ideologically to delegitimate women's interests or subordinate them to men's.'[28] As moral agents, as subjects of a public moral discourse, women will also create what Irigaray speaks of as 'a powerful female symbolic' and so radically alter the present ethical status of women. Those women who have the privilege and the possibility to shape the public ethical discourse must remain constantly vigilant of the extraordinary differences between and among women. While there may be some few issues upon which we can speak using the collective feminist 'we', we must ensure that our words do not dominate those who have not yet found their voice. Sarah Kofman, the great French philosopher who died in 1994, constantly challenged that we take words seriously and suggests 'in writing one must leave a space for the silence of those who could not speak: that is writing "without power" '.[29] A feminist ethical discourse must be 'without power' in this sense.

28 Alison M. Jagger, 'Feminist Ethics: Projects, Problems, Prospects', in Claudia Card (ed.), *Feminist Ethics*, (University Press of Kansas, 1991), p. 90.

29 Words taken from an interview with Sarah Kofman titled 'Writing Without Power', *Women's Philosophy Review* No. 13 (June 1995), p. 5.

A Feminist Ethics of Love

As one way of developing a model of ethics that integrates the ethics of the male and female imagination, I suggest that we re-establish, re-invent an ethics of love. As I have indicated earlier, imagination is at the heart of our capacity to hold opposites in creative tension and is therefore key in any move towards a more integrative model of ethics. To re-invent an ethics of love, to creatively image ways of loving justly and carefully is an imaginative act.

The re-invention of an ethic of love calls for women as well as men to shape the public moral discourse. The male bias in the traditional articulation of the ethical canon must give way to the richness and complexity of women's subjectivities. Put otherwise, the formulation of a new ethic of love must be a joint enterprise, mutually engaging both women and men. The inclusion of women's subjectivities in shaping an ethic of love will not simply enlarge and expand our understanding, but will in fact transform ethics as we know it today. This will be a complex and an ongoing task. For now, I can only begin to sketch the contours of such a dream.

An Ethics of Self-Love

Rooted in a feminist imagination, an ethics of love challenges us to take seriously the radical connection between love and action. The action of love begins firstly with the self. As Julia Kristeva states, 'Love is the time and space in which "I" assumes the right to be extraordinary.'[30] In a patriarchal world order, where women are socialised to sacrifice the self in care of others, it is an extraordinary act to love the self justly and carefully. To be gentle with oneself, to take the time and space to nourish the self without fear of narcissistic excess, is the fulcrum to prising open our unique potential. My personal power can only be accessed through the action of self-love. To claim this ethic of self-love will be new for women who have been

30 Kristeva, *Tales of Love* (New York: Columbia University Press, 1987), p. 5.

enculturated and who have willingly co-operated by handing over the self in perpetual self-giving. Indeed, the weight of tradition separates women from the love of herself. Yet it is only in loving that I come to be who I am. Such an ethic of love turns the Cartesian dictum 'I think, therefore I am' on its head; or rather it recentres heart rather than head as the locus of human becoming and ethical being.

Self-love gives us the confidence to be guided by our own deep intuition, our creativity and imagination. I agree with Audre Lorde:

> When we live outside ourselves, and by that I mean on external directives only, rather than from our internal knowledge and needs, when we live away from those erotic guides from within ourselves, then our lives are limited by external and alien forms, and we conform to the needs of a structure that is not based on human need, let alone an individual's. But when we begin to live from within outward, in touch with the power of the erotic within ourselves, and allowing that power to inform and illuminate our actions upon the world around us, then we begin to be responsible to ourselves in the deepest sense.[31]

It is love of self that spurs us to discover our own subjectivity. It is love of self that ignites the ethical imagination in a loving way. It is love of self that provides the necessary courage and confidence to dream of different ways than what we have been given. Further, the practice of self-love is profoundly interconnected with our capacity to love others and to be loved.

An Ethics of Mutual Love

A love of self, the claiming of one's own subjectivity, opens the possibility for mutual relationships – in friendship and/or life-long commitment – that allow us to know and to love the other as other. The coming together

31 *Sister Outsider*, p. 58. In the powerful essay, 'Uses of the Erotic' Audre Lorde describes her understanding of the erotic, 'When I speak of the erotic, then, I speak of it as an assertion of the lifeforce of women; of that creative energy empowered, knowledge and use of which we are now reclaiming in our language, our history, our dancing, our loving, our work, our lives', p. 55.

in mutual relationship will open up an extraordinary resource which has been repressed in relationships of domination. This resource is the power of the erotic. Beverly Harrison reminds us: 'The love we want and need is deeply mutual love, love that has both the quality of a gift received and the quality of a gift given … mutual love is love in its deepest radicality.'[32] But again to know the other as other and ultimately to know the divine who is Love, is dependent on the solid base of love of self. When women and women, women and men, men and men, love from a base of secure self-love, in an atmosphere of delight and joy in the other as other, then the creative force which is the essence of human existence is released. We create and are created by the dynamic movement of mutual love.

The radical challenge to live related lives is not an optional extra within the human vocation. Rather it is integral to human being and human understanding. Put otherwise, to be human is to be in relationship. Truly mutual love leads to transformation which enables divine love not just to be glimpsed but to be experienced. Sharing the passion of love in its deepest meaning opens up revelations of divine love. Exploring such sensual embodied understandings of love will allow us to prune back the dead, sanitised versions of Christian love which we have inherited. It will also call us to remodel our symbols and discourse about divinity. A patriarchal father god, cast within the agape tradition, who loves benevolently and generously but who seeks no return, is not a helpful model to motivate and sustain mutual relations. Instead, a feminist ethics of love views the divine as holy mystery running through the veins of erotic energy.

An Ethics of Global Love

While love starts with the particular – and our capacity to love is profoundly influenced by how we each have been particularly loved – a

32 Beverly Wildung Harrison, *Making the Connections: Essays in Feminist Social Ethics*, ed. by Carol Robb (Boston: Beacon Press, 1985), p. 361.

feminist ethics of love must constantly call beyond the known, the familiar. To live justice rooted in relationship is to love the other as other with compassionate openness. To live with a listening heart is to care for and be cared for by those most different to ourselves. As I have outlined previously, it is imagination which empowers sympathy and compassion and which moves us to respond to the image of the other most in need, in order to discern appropriate action. Much of what passes for love is a subtle controlling of the loved one until they are simply a mirror image of the lover. This need to reduce all reality to 'the same' is an indicator of how much we fear difference.

Living in post-modern times, where there is a constant debunking of the notion of meaning and universal truth, as well as a rage against any claim of absolute certainty, the question arises: what will motivate a human response to the desolation of our time? Richard Kearney suggests that it is the ethical imagination that will sustain human responsiveness to the needs of the other as other.[33] In the face of a global crisis where two-thirds of our population of five billion people live in abject poverty, it is essential that the motivation to act for change is sustained. While questions of being and truth may be in flux in these post-modern times, questions of ethics must be addressed and acted on.

In an age of mass-mediated communication, paralysis seems the only response to the bombardment of images of human tragedy which parade our television screens. In the endless procession of suffering and misery, it is the imagination which holds us from despair and challenges us, in community, to creatively discern what concrete action we can and must take.

The ethical imagination must hold in tandem both local and global issues which call for action. Indeed, our genuine capacity to empathise with the needs of those whose image appears on our television screens from afar, is profoundly connected to our present commitment to the local issues of poverty and suffering in our midst. Put conversely, those who refuse to be touched by local oppression will hardly be moved by global despair. In my

33 Kearney, *Wake*, p. 361.

own experience, the Shanty Educational Project has completely transformed my middle-class consciousness. Standing in partnership with women who live daily the injustices of poverty has radically altered my way of living in the world and viewing global issues.

As we reflect on the challenge of living mutually, we cannot grant hegemony simply to human relationships. Rather, the call to live lives of mutual sustainment challenges our relationship to animal and plant life. As a vegetarian and someone committed to organic growing, I know from experience how countercultural this broader understanding of mutuality is. I am constantly amazed how the amount of love for domestic animals is so blatantly counterbalanced by a disinterested disrespect for the lives of animals who eventually grace our tables as 'meat' or 'roast'. Concern for animals in our private world must be extended by our willingness to engage and shape the public debate about animal welfare in general. Yet I am convinced that if the binary division between culture and nature is ever to be corroded we must re-imagine the profound interconnection of all reality. To love mutually calls us beyond the notion that 'man' or 'woman' is the master of the universe and has permission to treat other life forms violently and with disrespect. Ursula Le Guin reminds us of the paucity of the position of 'civilised' man, separated over and against the rest of reality:

> By climbing up into his head and shutting out every voice but his own, 'civilised man' has gone deaf. He can't hear the wolf calling him brother, not master, but brother. He can't hear the earth calling him child – not Father, but son. He hears only his own words making up the world. He can't hear the animals. They have nothing to say. Children babble and have to be taught how to climb up into their heads and shut the doors of perception. No use teaching women at all, they talk all the time of course, but never say anything. This is the myth of civilisation, embodied in the monotheisms which assign soul to man alone.[34]

The re-invention of an ethics of love calls for a critical reappraisal of the connected web of all forms of life.

34 Ursula Le Guin, *Buffalo Gals and Other Animal Presences* (New York: Penguin/New American Library, 1987), p. 11.

The Virtues of Love

To re-invent an ethics of love, an integrative ethic that calls for care rooted in rationality and justice rooted in relationship, we ought to promote and foster certain virtues. In the traditional understanding of ethics, the development of virtue is needed for proper moral living. To live in a manner disposed to choose and will the good, demands that we acquire certain virtues. An ethic that has failed to recognise sexual difference, as it fostered male dominance and an economy of the 'same', has ipso facto neglected certain virtues, negated others. Indeed, the four virtues which I will claim are central to a feminist ethic of love would hardly be mentioned at all within the official canon.

The Virtue of Feeling

One of the victims of the mind/body dichotomy has been the whole world of feelings and the emotions. As mind is elevated above body in the Platonic inheritance, feelings and emotions at best are squashed into one side or the other of the dualistic divide. And so in medieval philosophy we learn of the equation of feelings with the body, mere bodily sensations, and emotions with the mind, aspects of the higher intellectual life. If we view the human being as a complex interconnection of mind-body-emotion-spirit, then the neat simplicity of the former interpretative framework collapses. Far from being simply an aspect of mind or body, our emotional life is a central aspect of who we are and who we can become. It also calls in question the emotion/feelings dichotomy. As Morwenna Griffiths challenges, we must 'take into consideration both physical and intelligent aspects of feelings.'[35] She continues: 'Far from feelings being seen as mere subjectivity, something to be overcome in the search for objectivity, they are seen to be a source of knowledge.'[36] As I indicated in the

35 Morvenna Griffiths and Margaret Whitford, eds. *Feminist Perspectives in Philosophy* (Indianapolis: Indiana University Press, 1988), p. 143.

36 Ibid, p. 135.

first chapter, feelings are central to a feminist pedagogy, the sharing of feelings/emotions within a group context is essential in women's journey towards self- understanding and self-knowledge. Furthermore, at the level of global awareness, our deep feeling about, for example, ecological devastation can move us to an understanding which acts for justice.

An ethics of love must be resourced by the virtue of feeling. To act for justice, to love with care, calls us beyond the stance of trying to control our feelings or seeking to dismiss our feelings and challenges us to touch deeply the well of feelings within. As I demonstrated earlier, the power of empathy, the ability to feel for and with the other as other, is a function of the imagination. Living in harmony with our feelings enhances our imaginative capacity and creative competency. The challenge to integrate emotion/feelings into public discourse remains. The time has come to question the heady discourse of patriarchy – a discourse severed from heart and thus from reality. The integration of emotion into the process of creating public policy will not breed weakness but rather will reveal a truth so far undisclosed. To quote Seams Heaney:

What looks the strongest has outlived its term;
The future lies with what's affirmed from under.

—The Canton of Expectations [37]

The onus lies with women to make visible and public the emotional dimension of human existence, 'to affirm from under' what has been silenced. By modelling diasporic values, values which have been driven into exile by the dominant discourse, much that has been lost could be recovered. The disruptive power of emotion – so feared by a male world which seeks to control and to dominate – could radically transform the ethical imagination and ultimately change the course of human history.

How many times have we heard: 'Let's keep feelings out of this!'? And, usually what is meant is, let's keep female feelings out of this. There is an intuitive sense in this prohibition of the revolutionary character of female emotion. Another way of fearing female emotion is to reduce it

37 In *New Selected Poems 1966–1987* (London: Faber and Faber, 1990), p. 237.

to stereotypical characteristics of 'femininity'. A way of experiencing the revolutionary character of female emotion, rather than theorising about it or reducing it, is to spend time with the artistic expression of the female emotion of Kathe Kollwitz, a German artist. Kathe Kollwitz, whose life embraced the political struggles of two centuries, must be remembered as a woman who broke open the definition of art. As a woman, she saw no distinction between her radical commitment to socialism and her gift as an artist. The historical experiences of her life are giving visibility with a rigorousness that evokes intense emotional response. It is impossible to view her lithographs without sharing the feelings expressed. As she herself stated, 'I have never been able to carry out any work coolly. On the contrary, it is done, so to speak, with my own blood.'[38] To re-invent an ethics of love is to practice the virtue of feeling.

The Virtue of Stillness

The radical commitment to an ethics of love calls each one of us to balance periods of action with periods of reflection. The challenge is to live tidally, that is, to be faithful to the ebb and flow of existence, interspersing prophetic action with mystical quiet.

To live love in its many dimensions is to foster the virtue of stillness. As Julia Kristeva reminds us: 'Love and soul cannot be disassociated.'[39] The love of self of which I spoke is impossible without giving oneself psychic space. To go within, to touch our creative self, necessitates entering the background of our lives. Luce Irigaray reminds us: 'Living requires knowing

38 *Kathe Kollwitz: Graphics, Posters, Drawings*, ed. Renate Hinz (NY: Pantheon Books, 1981), p. xvi.

39 *Tales of Love*, p. 63. Kristeva elaborates on this connection between love and contemplation later on in *Tales of Love*: 'Love is, in short the soul's sight for invisible things: contemplation triggers emotion, but it is possible to experience feelings (and the soul does in fact experience them) even for invisible beauties; any soul, so to speak does so, but especially the most "loving"', p. 110.

how to stop, reflect and even contemplate, so that we can become capable of situating ourselves individually and collectively.'[40]

The homelessness of spirit fed by consuming commercialism mars many lives. George Herbert summarises the situation well:

> my soul lay out of sight
> Untun'd, unstrung,
> My feeble spirit
> Like a nipt blossome, hung
> Discontented. [41]

To come home to the soul, to the power of the inner self is to enter daily a period of solitude. Some years ago in conversation with Aboriginal women in Australia, I learned of a tradition 40,000 years new which supports this idea. They spoke of a form of mysticism called 'dadirri'. It is inner, quiet listening and still awareness. Dadirri recognises the deep spring that is inside. There is no need to reflect too much or to do a lot of thinking. It is just being aware.[42] Siddhartha Gautama touched into this ancient tradition of awareness when, around 528 BCE, he articulated his understanding of Dhamma. Deep inner peace will enter the human condition only by engaging a practice of 'still awareness'. His empirical observation of human distress and constant mental agitation led him to a theory that notes the profound interconnection between bodily, mental, emotional and spiritual life. We live in a vicious circle of agitation between what we call the conscious and unconscious mind, or the mind and the deeper mind. This follows a sequence:

(1) the conscious mind perceives a stimulus, via the senses or via a thought arising;

40 *Thinking the Difference: For a Peaceful Revolution* (London: The Athlone Press, 1994), p. 34.

41 Extract from Deniall from *The Works of George Herbert*, Wordsworth Editions, (Hertfordshire, UK, 1994), p. 71.

42 See an article by Miriam Rose Ungunmerr-Baumann and Frank Brennan, 'Reverencing the Earth in the Australian Dreaming', *The Way* (January, 1989).

(2) the conscious mind identifies and judges it, assigning some negative or positive value (seemingly 'neutral' fragments are usually indifference rather than positive judgements);
(3) negative or positive sensations arise in or on the body with subtle or gross intensity in response to the intensity of the valuation, and
(4) the deep levels of the mind react to the (usually minute) bodily sensations by generating pleasant or unpleasant emotions or reactions.[43]

The practice of meditation seeks to interrupt this pattern of dissonance. In still awareness the conscious mind can break the spiral of agitation by allowing stimuli to simply come and go without engagement or valuation.

As Sogyal Rinpoche states:

> In the stillness and silence of meditation, we glimpse and return to that deep inner nature that we have so long lost sight of amid the busyness and distraction of our lives … Meditation, then, is bringing the mind home.[44]

Such an understanding of meditation where body, mind and spirit are profoundly connected, brings prayer back from the clouds and reminds us that, far from being an escape, it is a grounding renewal of the commitment to bring heaven to earth.

In recent years, I have taken up meditation and have found that the practice of 'still awareness' has changed my life. Listening to 'the news that is always arriving out of silence' (Rainer Maria Rilke in 'Duino elegies') has subtly transformed the way I perceive reality. Meditation is indeed a healing of body-mind-spirit-emotions. There is no one method of meditation and – as the Buddha himself insisted – the call to 'still awareness' lies outside any one religious tradition or ideology. As with all learning, practice will be accelerated by the acquisition of a good teacher.

43 I am indebted to Charlene Spretnak in her excellent chapter on Buddhism in *States of Grace: The Recovery of Meaning in the Postmodern Age*, for this concise statement, p. 39.

44 Sogyal Rinpoche, *Meditation* (London: Rider, Ebuyr Press, 1994, pp. 12–13.

Within his own teaching, Siddhartha Gautama believed that living morally was interdependent with the practice of meditation and both of these lead to wisdom. I agree that the virtue of stillness, the practice of quiet reflection, is essential if we are to sustain our commitment to an ethic of love. What else could sustain us 'daring to live for the impossible'! (Muriel Rukeyser)

Like the virtue of feeling, the practice of 'still awareness' is an imaginative act.

Integral to the practice of meditation is what I will call the mystical imagination. It is the imagination which frees us from the givens of present reality and allows us open to the beyond in our midst. One of the marks of the mystical tradition within Christianity is the presence of vivid imaginations. I think of Hildegarde of Bingen and her *Illuminations*[45] and of Julian of Norwich and her *Revelations of Divine Love*.[46] The writings and teachings of these women are testimony to the fertility of imagination which was integral to their lives. Imagery and symbolism permeate their work, acting as a bridge between heaven and earth and calling to depths of insight. Theirs is a spirituality of 'still awareness' which weaves transcendence and immanence, soul and body, divine, human and cosmic in ways unknown in classical theological texts. Prayer is clearly the practice of relatedness, taking the time and the space to retrieve the essence of what existence is about; living relatedly. In one of her mystical experiences, Hildegarde describes being raised up and spread out among different peoples who were far away from her in distant lands. In one of Julian's revelations the whole universe appears, reduced to the size of a hazelnut. As she gazes on this object, so small yet so perfectly formed, she is overwhelmed both by a sense of the fragility of all earthly existence but also by a deep appreciation for the Divine mystery who sustains all life. 'It lasts and always will because

45 For a very readable and beautifully illustrated version of the *Illuminations* with text by Hildegarde of Bingen and commentary by Matthew Fox, see the production from New Mexico: Bear & Company, 1985).

46 *Revelations of Divine Love* are taken from Edmond Colledge, O. S. A. and James Walsh, S. J. *Julian of Norwich: Shewings The Classics of Western Spirituality* (Paulist Press, 1978).

God loves it; and thus everything has been through the love of God.'[47] It is imagination that allows us to weave connections in moments of mystical quiet between aspects of reality which otherwise would remain disparate.

It is clear from what has been stated that the practice of 'still awareness' is not an exercise of mind severed from body. Rather, entering our centre allows us to enter our heart space and experience at a very deep level the integration of mind-body-emotion- spirit. (Vipassana meditation, for example, is rooted in gentle attentiveness to the body, sensations and to different states of mind.[48]). Most practices of meditation commence with a period of quiet attention to breathing, the life force that links mind and body.

It must also be stated that the practice of meditation is not a naval gazing exercise undertaken by self-indulgent and narcissistic types. Nor is it a practice in self-preoccupation where the vision of one's world is limited to the boundaries of the self. Catherine Keller describes it this way:

> It is a stillness born of a greater width of connection, from a livelier attunement to being here now, from my body's presence to its surrounding cosmos. The calm distils itself from the subtle bustle of all things in process. Getting centred, we feel the sudden warmth of the deeper desire – even of what mystics call the 'heart's desire'. A desire that leads us beyond ourselves – to selves both new and other.[49]

The virtue of stillness, the practice of mystical quiet must accompany the prophetic stance against injustices. To avoid burn out, to stay the pace, we must constantly return to the 'fountain of life' (Hildegarde) and drink deep of the waters.

The Virtue of Embodiment

An ethic of love challenges that we bring our entire selves to the radical work of justice and care. In order to do this, we must reclaim our bodies

47 Julian of Norwich, *Revelations of Divine Love*, Short Text, chapter 4.

48 For those interested in this form of meditation, see *Vipassana Newsletter* Dhamma Dipa Harewood End, Hereford, HR2 8NG, UK.

49 Catherine Keller, *From a Broken Web*, p. 213.

as central to all moral knowledge and action.[50] As Beverly Harrison argues, 'All our knowledge including our moral knowledge, is body mediated.'[51]

To practice the virtue of embodiment calls us firstly to critique the moral tradition that we have inherited – culturally constructed solely by men – which has undermined the place of the body in ethics. Rooted in the Platonic dualism which elevated mind over body, moral perfection could only be achieved by escaping from the ways of the flesh. The body was mortified, flagellated, even sacrificed to the transcendent call of the rational good. This body/mind dualism was rooted in clear gender delineations. As Aristotle put it quite blatantly: 'While the body is from the female, it is the soul that is from the male, for the soul is the reality (substance) of a particular body.'[52] The higher good is always disembodied, therefore, it is hardly surprising that patriarchal ethics seeks to suppress or at best control the body, and to equate women with the body.

The practice of the virtue of embodiment challenges both men and women to return to their bodies and to claim the respective difference of this homecoming. This will call for a correction to the male imagination which has equated the flesh with the female. Returning home from this objectification of the body to their own bodies, attending with gentle awareness to the corporeal roots of their being, should open the pores of sensibility to the unacceptability of violence. Our bodies need less mastery and control and more love and respectful attentiveness. The process of this homecoming will call men to re-examine the myths underpinning the macho stereotype and masculinity. The image of the 'masculine body' as strong, giving, active, as counterposed to the 'feminine body' as weak, receptive, passive, will be exposed as a delusion. As women and men cross

50 My concern with the embodiment of subjectivity is not an essentialist position which can be dismissed as a revamping of biological determinism, rather it is rooted in a deeply felt position that the body is the site for the intersection of thought and action, transcendence and immanence, the semiotic and the symbolic, the political and the aesthetic.

51 Beverly Harrison, *Making the Connections*, p. 13.

52 *Genesis of Animals* A, 735 A 14–16.

the threshold to a new acceptance of their own bodiliness, and relate from a premise of mutual nourishment, the recognition will dawn that we are in fact both 'actively receptive.'[53]

Women, for their part, must engage in resurrecting their bodies from a patriarchal history of objectification, denigration, even abuse. They must question a tradition which distorts logic and places 'word' before 'flesh', and honours sacrifice more highly than birth. Cixoux challenges all women: 'Your body is yours, take it.'[54] Or as Paula Meehan, a young Irish poet in her poem titled 'Home' writes:

> The wise women say you must live in your skin, call *it* home,
> no matter how battered or broken, misused by the world, you can heal.[55]

The journey home to our bodies, our real selves, must take place in both the personal and the public spheres. More and more women are aware that we must live embodied lives if we are to touch our most creative source. To really love the self is to reclaim our bodiliness. But few have brought this awareness to the public arena where ethical decisions are made and moral resolutions are shaped. A return to our bodies allows us firstly to recognise that all knowledge is rooted in our bodiliness. A second step in this awareness is to name clearly that the moral normativity which we have inherited, with all its claims to objectivity and transcendence, is in fact rooted in male experience and is an expression of male bodiliness. Such a perspective flies in the face of the inherited logic, which entirely separated the thinking mind from the feeling body. Take for example Descartes reflection in the 'Sixth Meditation':

> On the one hand I have a clear and distinct idea of myself, so far as I am simply a thinking, non-extended thing and on the other hand I have a distinct idea of body,

53 Margaret Farley, 'New Patterns of Relationship: Beginnings of a Moral Revolution', *Theological Studies* 1975, p. 279.

54 Helene Cixoux, 'The Laugh of Medusa', translated K. & P. Cohen, Signs 1 (1): 876.

55 Paula Meehan, 'Home', from *As if By Magic: Selected Poems* (Dublin: Daedalus Press, 2020).

> insofar as this is simply extended non-thinking thing. And accordingly it is certain that I am really distinct from my body and can exist without it.[56]

A feminist ethics of love gives no further credence to the lie of separation from and suspicion of the body. Rather, it calls both men and women to honestly recognise that we think through the body, and that our ethics recognises sexual difference. Indeed an ethics that would allow female and male embodiment to find public voice, encouraging the expression of the mutual difference inherent in each subjectivity, would be a different ethics to any that has yet been articulated. Returning to the body, to the corpo(real) could open us to an understanding of reality hitherto unglimpsed. 'Just ask yourselves', Irigary urges, 'whether the Real might not be some very repressed-censored-forgotten "thing" to do with the body.'[57]

It is clear that each of the virtues which I have mentioned are interconnected with each other. Reinventing an ethics of love to ensure that 'our courage will not fail our love'[58] challenges us to live lives in touch with our feelings, rooted in our bodiliness and committed to 'still awareness.' To conclude this very personal exhortation to virtue which makes no claims to being exhaustive, I wish to reflect on one more virtue. This is my belief that the virtue of wonder is the canvas on which the aforementioned tapestry is woven.

The Virtue of Wonder

A short story I have loved for years is called 'The Windows of Wonder'.[59] Rereading the story today, I was yet again moved to tears by the power and

56 Rene Descartes, 'Sixth Meditation', from *The Philosophical Writings of Descartes* 2 Vols. ed. John Cottingham et al. (Cambridge: Cambridge University Press), p. 76.

57 Luce Irigaray, 'The poverty of Psychoanalysis', trans. David Macey with Margaret Whitford in *The Irigaray Reader*, ed. Margaret Whitford (Oxford: Blackwell), p. 86.

58 Sharon Welch, *A Feminist Ethics of Risk.*

59 See Bryan MacMahon, 'The Windows of Wonder', in *Exploring English: Anthology of Short Stories* (Dublin: Gill & Macmillan, Ltd., 1967) pp. 144–150.

the insight of the narrative. A young teacher has been given a temporary job in a small rural school set within a dark valley. The little children who are placed in her charge are as inert as the stones in the nearby fields. She's been forewarned: 'They will eat you with their big brown eyes.' Trying every and any unorthodox method from leaping to laughing, from music to mimicry, she cannot find the secret to these children's natures and all her efforts are greeted with blank disinterest. One day, quite by accident, she asked them if they knew the story of the 'Children of Lir'. When silence greeted her question she listed many other stories in the Irish tradition. No, they were unfamiliar with this whole world. Holding back her tears she quickly gathered them around, 'Please try to understand: How shall I begin to tell you of the treasure you have lost? Your minds are like rooms that are dark or brown. But somewhere in the room, if only you can pull aside the heavy curtains, you will find windows of wonder.' The story continues and ends very beautifully. It reminds us of an age-old truth, namely, that the capacity to wonder is central to living the human vocation creatively, passionately – ever open to the surprise of life.

Like Bryan Mac Mahon with this simple story, Luce Irigaray, in more philosophical language, bemoans the passing of this virtue: 'There is no window, no sense remaining open on, or with, the world, the Other, the other. In order to dwell within it, transform it. What is lacking there in terms of the passions is wonder.'[60]

Put positively, wonder is the root of all virtue and must be cultivated if we are to re-invent an ethics of love. Indeed, Descartes spoke of wonder as the first of all the passions:

> When the first encounter with some object surprises us, and we judge it to be new or very different from what we formerly knew, or from what we supposed that it ought to be that causes us to wonder and be surprised and because that may happen before we in any way know whether this object is agreeable to us or is not so, it appears to me that wonder is the first of all the passions.[61]

60 Luce Irigaray, *An Ethics of Sexual Difference*, p. 73.

61 Rene Descartes, *The Passions of the Soul*, art 53, p. 358. as quoted by Luce Irigaray in her excellent chapter on Wonder: A Reading of Descartes, The Passions of the soul, in *An Ethics of Sexual Difference*, p. 73.

It is the capacity to wonder that holds us open allowing us to be surprised by difference, engaged by the beauty of diversity. Far from desiring to reduce all reality to sameness or oneness, wonder thrives on strangeness, delights in difference.

Our ability to wonder allows us to live with the 'excess' of the other, and not to reduce the other to a mere reflection of oneself. Rather, wonder allows their otherness to be. Our ability to wonder opens onto, and finds expression in, our capacity to affirm, namely, self-affirmation and also the genuine and explicit naming of the good in the other. In a world riddled with jealously and envy, the transformative power of affirmation must never be underrated. Furthermore, the practice of the virtue of wonder from our earliest years could heal our tendency to destruction and violence. If we really revere the other as other and remain open rather than threatened by their difference, then a culture of violence would no longer be acceptable.

The practice of the passion of wonder permeates all our relationships, not simply to others but also to the world and to that which we recognise as divine mystery. Furthermore, it is the pre-condition for maintaining mutuality within these different relationships. To relate in wonderment, ever open to being surprised also shapes the self. To be able to respond with wonder reflects a capacity to be able to live in the now, a willingness to change when change is needed. I remember a story told to me by a Sr. Agnes in the twilight of her life, a story that illustrates that children above all can teach us about the eternal newness of existence. In the simplicity of their gestures and words, in the openness of their hearts, children can place before us images of the possible:

> Molly, a girl child aged seven, sat in the state classroom of Sr. Agnes, a very severe primary school educator. Despite her best efforts Sr. Agnes could not get Molly to conform. One day, Sr. Agnes recalls being deliberately cruel and she really put Molly in her place with a number of caustic remarks. Molly was silenced at last, she thought. An hour later it was break time, and the children filed into the yard. Sr. Agnes was arranging things on her desk when suddenly she felt a little hand in hers. 'Sister', whispered Molly, 'why don't you come out and play?' Sr. Agnes narrated that, that moment, those words, changed her life. After class that day she went to the convent chapel and there she remained until the following morning. During this vigil of conversion she watched the journey of her life pass before her eyes. Filled with the love of God and youthful enthusiasm and dedication, she had entered a Religious

> order to give her life to the education of children. However, over the years, she had become entirely institutionalised, legalistic and hard-hearted. Molly's gesture of love had broken through the encrustation of the years and had awakened her heart to wonder. Returning to the classroom, gradually she changed from being a teacher who kept control to one who cared and loved. Surprised by love in the words of this little girl, Agnes' life changed utterly.

The first passion, wonder, is integral to the virtue of feeling as I have indicated. But wonder is also present in the practice of the virtue of stillness. Again, Luce Irigaray suggests that 'Wonder would be the passion of the encounter between the most material and the most metaphysical of their possible conception and fecundation one by the other.'[62] The preamble to the practice of 'still awareness' is surely the capacity to wonder. The capacity to recognise the more in the now, the eternal in the present, opens in us the desire to dwell in stillness with life's gracious giftedness.

Finally, the virtue of wonder intermeshes with the virtue of embodiment. Our capacity to wonder is commensurate with our sense of embodiment. Windows of wonder open on the world from the home of embodiment. Our body-self is the space, the place from which we move in wonder and affirmation of life's gift.

Conclusion

To re-invent an ethics of love, an ethics rooted in and resourced by a feminist imagination, we must deliberately act for justice and live with care through different types of love. Lives committed to action for transformation must be resourced by the practice of virtues. Our ethical vision for a world where difference dwells in mutuality must be sustained by an imagination which constantly creates images of the possible through images of utopia. A community of love – of solidarity amidst difference – is the setting of such re-invention and ethical imaginings.

[And, it still is, twenty some years on.]

62 *Ibid.*, p. 82.

APPENDIX A

Exercise 1: Conducted within a Group Context

- Ask each woman to attend carefully to all the images of women which surround her present life – local billboards, magazines and newspaper imagery, television advertisements, videos, TV soaps, etc.
- List the images that evoke a response, whether positive or negative.
- Name the feelings that come up as one dwells with any one image.
- What image affirms your experience as a woman at this time, at this age, as part of this race, as living in this place?
- Select one or two images that you find self-affirming, journal with these images.
- If possible, get copies of these images and put them up in your home or workplace.
- As a group decide on the political action that should be taken in relation to images which denigrate, deny or undermine our self-defined subjectivity.

I have found that this exercise, which can take place over a few weeks, shifts any feeling of inertia about the power of imagery. Furthermore, it allows women to name the fact that if personal and social transformation to take place, if we are to move towards a world of mutual relations, then attention to imagery is at the heart of the matter.

Appendix B

Facilitate this exercise within a group context. Conduct it in light of our study on 'sexual difference', on the challenge to women to claim their own subjectivity as 'mutual other'.

A World of Mutual Relations

- Request each woman in the group to write down a goal that she would like to see achieved in the social and economic order thirty years from now. This goal should reflect the theme: 'A World of Mutual Relations'.
- Now return to your past. Choose an experience of 'mutual relations' from your past life that you would enjoy re-living and that you would be willing to share with others. Recall this experience in detail: the people involved, the emotions felt, the smells, colours, the location etc. Jot down some details of this memory. Then share in groups of four.
- Now take an imaginary journey into the future. Imagine thirty years from now.

  This is an exercise of focused or intentional imagining. Just relax and observe the world that gradually comes into focus in your imagination: look, record … remain open. Move around in this future world, talk to people you encounter. What are they doing? … the children, the women, the men. How are the animals treated? What is the state of the environment? What kinds of household groupings are there? What is the educational system like? What religious institutions or spirituality groups are present? Make notes and sketches of what you find.

- Now tell the others in your small group what you found. Just listen to each other – don't judge or compare – just ask questions for clarification when necessary.
- Next within your group take a large sheet of paper and draw the central images, symbols of your future world, combing the various viewpoints. Then state how this world is structured, how institutions function. In particular how power is used and how conflict is managed.
- Now standing in this future world – this world of mutual relations – work backwards, five years at a time, back to 2003 and chronicle how the world got to where it is now.
- Back in 2003 what short-term planning should we engage in so as to achieve a world of mutual relations?

This exercise combines work with memory and imagination in a very deliberate way. Memory work can be more easily approached and can often give confidence to engage in the work of creatively imagining the future. The exercise is an example of how intellect, emotion and imagination can function within a mutual embrace.

Bibliography

Amsberg, Kiki, and Steentiuis, Aafke. 'An Interview with Luce Irigaray'. Translated by Robert van Krieken. *Hecate 9* (1983).

Aristotle. *De Anima.*

——. *Genesis of Animals.*

——. *De Santa Virginitate.*

——. *De Trinitate.*

Bachelard, G. *Poetics of Space*. Translated by Maria Jolas. Boston, MA: Beacon Press, 1964.

Beaton, Catherine. "Does the Church Discriminate Against Women on the Basis of Their Sex?" *Critic* (June-July 1966).

Boff, Clodovis. *Praxis and Theology: Epistemological Foundations*. Maryknoll, NY: Orbis, 1987.

Boland, Eavan. 'The Art of Grief.' In *A Time of Violence*. Manchester: Carcanet Press, 1994, p. 52.

——. *Object Lessons. The Life of the Woman & the Poet in Our Time*. Manchester: Carcanet Press, 1995.

Børreson, Kari. *Subordination and Equivalence: The Nature and Role of Woman in Augustine and Thomas Aquinas*. Washington, DC: University Press of America, 1981.

Braidotti, Rosi. 'The Politics of Ontological Difference'. In *Between Feminism and Psychoanalysis*. Edited by Theresa Brennan. London: Routledge, 1989.

——. *Patterns of Dissonance. A Study of Women in Contemporary Philosophy*. Translated by Elizabeth Guild. London: Polity Press, 1991.

——. *Nomadic Subjects*. New York: Columbia University Press, 1993.

Brann, Eva T. H. *The World of the Imagination: Sun and Substance*. Maryland: Rowman & Littlefield Publisher, Inc., 1991.

Buber, Martin. *I and Thou*. Translated by Walter Kaufman. New York: Charles Scribner's Sons, 1970.

Cameron, Deborah. *Feminism and Linguistic Theory*. London: Macmillan, 1985.

Casey, Edward. *Imagining: A Phenomenological Study*. Indiana University Press, 1979.

Chanter, Tina. *Ethics of Eros: Irigaray's Rewriting of the Philosophers*. New York: Routledge, 1995.

Christ, Carol P. *Laughter of Aphrodite: Reflections on a Journey to the Goddess*. San Francisco: Harper & Row Publishers, 1987.

Cixous, Helene. 'The Laugh of the Medusa'. Translated by K & P Cohen. *Signs* 1/1 (1976): 875–99.

Coleridge, Samuel Taylor. *Statesman's Manual.* Edited by R. J. White. 1816.

Coleridge, Samuel Taylor. *Biographia Literaria.* Edited by J. Shawcross. Oxford: Oxford University Press, 1907.

Coles, Robert. *The Call Of Stories. Teaching and The Moral Imagination.* Boston: Houghton, Mifflin Company, 1989.

Condren, Mary. *The Serpent and the Goddess: Women, Religion & Power in Celtic Ireland.* San Francisco: Harper & Row, 1989.

Cooey, Paula M. *Religious Imagination and the Body.* New York: Oxford University Press, 1994.

Cook, Patricia, ed. *Philosophical Imagination and Cultural Memory.* Durham: Duke University Press, 1993.

Cornell, Drucilla. *Beyond Accommodation. Ethical Feminism, Deconstruction, & the Law.* London: Routledge, 1991.

Crawford, June, Kippax, Susan, Onyx, Jenny, Gault, Una and Benton, Pam. *Emotion and Gender. Constructing Meaning from Memory.* London: Sage Publications, 1992.

Crawford, Mary. *Talking Difference. On Gender and Language.* London: Sage Publications, 1995.

Cummins, Pauline and Walsh, Louise. See notes published by the Irish Museum of Modern Art to accompany the exhibition. *Sounding the Depths* 1 April – 9th May 1992.

Daly, Mary in cahoots with Jane Caputi. *Gyn/Ecology: The Metaethics of Radical Feminism.* Boston: Beacon Press, 1978.

de Brun, Mary O'Reilly. *From Silence to Sacred Speech: An Exploration in Feminist Spirituality.* MA thesis for Maynooth, 1992.

Descartes, Rene. *The Philosophical Writings of Descartes.* 2 Vols. Edited by John Cottingham et al. Cambridge: Cambridge University Press.

Doeuff, Michel Le. *The Philosophical Imaginary.* London: The Athlone Press Ltd., 1989.

Downes, Paul and Gilligan, Ann Louise. *Beyond Educational Disadvantage.* Dublin: Institute of Public Affairs, 2007.

Eisenstein, Zillah. *The Radical Future of Liberal Feminism.* Boston: Northeastern University Press, 1981.

Eliot, T. S. 'East Coker', from *Four Quartets.* In *Collected Poems 1909–1962*, pp. 196–204. London: Faber and Faber Ltd., 1965.

Engell, James. *The Creative Imagination: Enlightenment to Romanticism.* Cambridge: Harvard University Press, 1981.

Evans, Judith. *Feminist Theory Today. An Introduction to Second-Wave Feminism.* London: Sage Publications, 1995.

Farley, Margaret. 'New Patterns of Relationship: Beginnings of a Moral Revolution'. *Theological Studies* (1975).

Fiorenza, Elisabeth Schüssler. 'Towards a Liberating and a Liberated Theology: Women Theologians and Feminist Theology in the USA'. In *Doing Theology in New Place*. Edited by Jossua and Metz. Concilium 1155. New York: Seabury, 1979.

Freire, Paolo. *Pedagogy of the Oppressed*. New York: The Seabury Press, 1970.

Freyne, Gail Grossman. *From Equal Object to Different Subject: The Quest for Women's Identity Within Marriage*. MA thesis in Women's Studies, UCD, 1994.

Friel, Brian. *Brian Friel: Plays 1*. London: Faber and Faber, 1996, pp. 377–451.

Gardner, Howard. *Art, Mind and Brain*. New York: Basic Books, Inc., 1982.

Gilligan, Ann Louise and Zappone, Katherine. *Our Lives Out Loud: In Pursuit of Justice and Equality*. Dublin: O'Brien Press, 2008.

Gimbutas, Marija. *The Goddesses and Gods of Old Europe 6500–3500. Myths & Images*. Berkeley: University of California Press, 1989.

——. *The Language of the Goddess*. San Francisco: Harper & Row, 1989.

Gore, Jennifer M. *The Struggle for Pedagogies*. New York: Routledge, 1993.

Green, Maxine. *Teacher as Stranger*.

Griffiths, Morvenna, and Whitford, Margaret, eds. *Feminist Perspectives in Philosophy*. Indianapolis: Indiana University Press, 1988.

Groome, Thomas H. *Christian Religious Education: Sharing Our Story and Vision*. San Francisco: Harper and Row, 1980.

Harding, Michael. 'Misogynist'. In *The Crack in the Emerald: New Irish Plays*. London: Nick Hern Books, 1990, pp. 141–88.

Harding, Sandra, and Hintikka, Merrill, eds. *Introduction to Discovering Reality: Feminist Perspectives on Epistemology, Metaphysics, Methodology & Philosophy of Science*. Pordrecht, Holland: D. Reidel, 1983.

Harrision, Beverly Wildung. *Making the Connections: Essays in Feminist Social Ethics*, Edited by Carol Robb. Boston: Beacon Press, 1985.

Hart, Ray. *Unfinished Man and the Imagination: Toward an Ontology and a Rhetoric of Revelation*. New York: Herder & Herder, 1968.

Hartley, Ernest. *Anima Poetae*. Edited by Coleridge. London: William Heinenann, 1885.

Haughton, Rosemary. *Song in a Strange Land: The Wellspring Story and the Homelessness of Women*. Illinois: Templegate Publishers, 1991.

Heaney, Seamus. 'From the Canton of Expectations' In *New Selected Poems 1966–1987*. London: Faber and Faber, 1990, p. 237.

Heaney, Seamus. *Seeing Things*. London: Faber and Faber, 1991.

Heyward, Carter. *Touching Our Strength: The Erotic as Power and the Love of God*. San Francisco: Harper & Row, 1989.

Hildegarde of Bingen. *Illuminations*. Commentary by Matthew Fox. New Mexico: Bear & Company, 1985.

Hirsch, Marianne. *The Mother-daughter Plot: Narrative, Psychoanalysis, Feminism*. Bloomington: Indiana University Press, 1989.

Holden, Pat, ed. *Women's Religious Experience*. London: Croom Helm, 1983.

Hooks, Bell. *Teaching To Transgress. Education as the Practice of Freedom*. New York: Routledge, 1994.

Hume, David. *A Treatise of Human Nature*. Edited by L. A. Selby-Bigge. Oxford: Clarendon Press, 1967.

Hume, David. *Treatise (Of the Passions)*.

Irigaray, Luce. 'Women's Exile: Interview with Luce Irigaray'. *Ideology and Consciousness* (1977).

——. *Parler n 'est jamais neutre*. Paris: Minuit, 1985.

——. *Speculum of the Other Woman*. Translated by Gillian G. Gill. Ithaca: Cornell University Press, 1985.

——. *This Sex Which Is Not One*. Translated by Catherine Porter. Ithaca: Cornell University Press, 1985.

——. 'Sexual Difference'. In *French Feminist Thought: A Reader*.

——. 'The Bodily Encounter with the Mother'. In *The Irigaray Reader*. Edited by Margaret Whitford. London: Basil Blackwell, 1991.

——. 'The Poverty of Psychoanalysis'. In *The Irigaray Reader*. Edited by Margaret Whitford. Translated by David Macey with Margaret Whitford. London: Basil Blackwell, 1991.

——. 'Women-Mothers, the Silent Substratum of the Social Order'. In *The Irigaray Reader*. Translated by David Macey. Edited by Margaret Whitford. Oxford: Blackwell, 1991.

——. *Elemental Passions*. Translated by Joanne Collie & Judity Still. London: The Athlone Press, 1992.

——. *An Ethics of Sexual Difference*. New York: Cornell University, 1993.

——. 'Divine Woman'. In *Sexes and Genealogies*. New York: Columbia University Press, 1993.

——. *Je, tu, nous: Towards a Culture of Difference*. Translated by Alison Martin. New York: Routledge, 1993.

——. *Sexes and Genealogies*. Translated by Gillian Gill. New York: Columbia University Press, 1993.

——. *Thinking the Difference: For a Peaceful Revolution*. London: The Athlone Press, 1994.

Jagger, Alison M. 'Feminist Ethics: Projects, Problems, Prospects'. In *Feminist Ethics*. Edited by Claudia Card. Lawrence, Kansas: University Press of Kansas, 1991.

Jardine, Alice, and Menke, Anne, eds. *Shifting Scenes: Interviews on Women, Writing and Politics in Post '68 France*. New York: Columbia University Press, 1991.

John Paul II, 'Apostolic Letter on Ordination and Women'. *Origins* Vol. 24, No. 4 (June 9 1994).

Johnson, Elizabeth. *She Who Is: The Mystery of God in Feminist Theological Discourse*. New York: Crossroad, 1992.

Johnson, Mark. *Moral Imagination: Implications of Cognitive Science for Ethics*. Chicago: The University of Chicago Press, 1993.

Julian of Norwich. *Revelations of Divine Love*. In *Julian of Norwich: Shewings*. Translated and edited by Edmond Colledge, O. S. A. and James Walsh, S. J. New York: Paulist Press, 1978.

Kaminski, Phyllis H. 'Kristevas and the Cross: Rereading the Symbol of Redemption'. In *Women and Theology*. Edited by Mary Ann Hinsdale and Phyllis H. Kaminski. New York: Orbis Books, 1995.

Kanfer, Stephen. 'Sispeak'. *Time* 23 October 1972.

Kant, Immanuel. *Critique of Judgement*.

Kant, Immanuel. *Transcendental Deduction*. Translated by Norman Kemp Smith. London: Macmillan, 1929.

Kaplan, Cora. 'Language and Gender'. In *Papers on Patriarchy. Women's Publishing Collective*, 1976.

Kaufmann, Gordon. *The Theological Imagination: Constructing the Concept of God*. Philadelphia: Westminster Press, 1981.

Kearney, Richard. *Dialogues with Contemporary Thinkers*. Manchester: Manchester University Press, 1984.

——. *The Wake of Imagination: Ideas of Creativity in Western Culture*. London: Hutchinson, 1988

——. *Poetics of Imagining: From Husserl to Lyotard*. London: Harper Collins Academic, 1991.

——. *Poetics of Modernity: Towards a Hermeneutic Imagination*. New Jersey: Humanities Press, 1995.

——. *States of Mind*. Manchester: Manchester University Press, 1995.

Keller, Catherine. *From a Broken Web. Separation, Sexism, and Self*. Boston: Beacon Press, 1986.

Keller, Catherine. *Apocalypse New & Then: A Feminist Guide to the End of The World*. Boston: Beacon Press, 1996.

Khatena, Joe. *Imagery and Creative Imagination*. Buffalo, NY: Beady and Creative Education Foundation, 1984.

——. 'Research Potential of Imagery and Creative Imagination'. In *Frontiers of Creativity Research: Beyond the Basics*. Edited by S. G. Isaksen. Buffalo, NY: Beady, 1986.

Knox, John. *An Inclusive-Language Lectionary Year A.* Westminster and Pilgrim Presses, 1983–1986.

Kofman, Sarah. 'Writing Without Power'. *Women's Philosophy Review* No. 13.

Kramarae, C. *Women and Men Speaking:Frameworks for Analysis.* Rowley, MA: Newbury House Publishers, 1981.

Kristeva, Julia. *Tales of Love.* New York: Columbia University Press, 1987.

Lacan, Jacques. *The Language of the Self: The Function of Language in Psychoanalysis.* Translated by Anthony Wilden. Baltimore: John Hopkins University Press, 1968.

LaCugna, Catherine Mowry. *God for Us: The Trinity and Christian Life.* New York: HarperCollins, 1991.

Lawlor, Leonard. *Imagination and Chance, The Difference Between the Thought of Ricoeur and Derrida.* New York: State University of New York Press, 1992.

Le Guin, Ursula. *The Eye of the Heron.* New York: Harper and Row, 1978.

——. *Always Coming Home.* New York: Bantam Books, 1987.

——. *Buffalo Gals and Other Animal Presences.* New York: Penguin/New American Library, 1987.

——. *Dancing At the Edge of the World.* New York: Grove Press, 1989.

Lessing, Doris. *Landlocked.* London: MacGibbon & Kee, 1965.

Lewis, Magda Gere. *Without A Word. Teaching Beyond Women's Silence.*

Lorde, Audre. *Sister Outsider: Essays and Speeches.* New York: The Crossing Press Feminist Series, 1984, pp. 38–39.

Lorde, Audre. *The Marvelous Arithmetics of Distance Poems 1987–1992.* New York: W.W. Norton & Company, 1993.

MacMahon, Bryan. 'The Windows of Wonder'. In *Exploring English: Anthology of Short Stories.* Dublin: Gill & Macmillan, Ltd., 1967.

Madison, Gary. *The Hermeneutics of Postmodernity: Figures and Themes.* Bloomington: Indiana University Press, 1990.

Mahon, Derek. 'Everything is Going to Be All Right'. *Selected Poems.* London: Viking/Gallery, 1991.

McDaniel, J. *Reconstituting the World: The Poetry and Vision of Adrienne Rich.* Argyle: New York Spinsters Inc., 1978.

McIntyre, John. *Faith Theology and Imagination.* Edinburgh: The Handsel Press, 1987.

Meehan, Paula. 'Home'. In *As If by Magic: Selected Poems.* Dublin: Daedalus Press, 2020.

Miles, Margaret. *Image as Insight. Visual understanding in Western Christianity & Secular Culture.* Boston: Beacon Press, 1985.

Miller, Casey, and Swift, Kate. *The Handbook of Non-Sexist Writing,* 2nd edn. London: The Women's Press, 1988.

Montague, John. 'A Grafted Tongue'. In *New Collected Poems* (2012) reproduced by kind permission of the author's estate and The Gallery Press.

Morton, Nelle. *The Journey Is Home*. Boston: Beacon Press, 1985.

Murdoch, Iris. *The Fire and the Sun: Why Plato Banished the Artists*. London: Oxford University Press, 1977.

Ní Dhomhnaill, Nuala. 'We Are Damned, My Sisters.' In *Selected Poems: Translated by Michael Hartnett*. Dublin: Raven Arts Press, 1988, p. 11.

Olivier, Christiane. *Jocasta's Children: The Imprint of the Mother.* London: Routledge, 1989.

Pellauer, Mary. 'Moral Callousness and Moral Sensitivity: Violence Against Women'. In *Women's Consciousness; Women's Conscience*. Edited by Barbara Hilkert Andolsen et al. Minneapolis: Winston Press, 1985.

Perpetua. 'The Martyrdom of Perpetua: A Protest Account of Third Century Christianity'. In *A Lost Tradition: Women Writers of the Early Church*. Edited by Patricia Wilson-Kastner et al. New York: University Press of America, 1981.

Piercy, Marge. *Circles on the Water*. New York: Alfred A. Knopf, 1986.

Pius XI. 'Casti Connubii, 1930'. In *The Woman in the Modem World: Papal Teachings*. Edited by Benedictine Monks of Solesines. Boston: St. Paul Editions, 1959.

Plato, *The Republic*. Translated with an introduction by A. D. Lindsay. London: J. M. Dent & Sons Ltd.

Power, Kim E. *Augustine's Theology of Women: Influences and Implications*, Thesis presented to Melbourne University. Reagan, Charles E., and Stewart, David. Boston. Beacon Press, 1978.

Regan, C., and Stewart, D., eds. *The Philosophy of Paul Ricoeur*. Boston: Beacon, 1973.

Rich, Adrienne. *A Wild Patience Has Taken me Thus Far. Poems 1978–1981*. New York. WW Norton & Co. 1981.

——. 'Planetarium.' In *The Fact of a Doorframe: Poems Selected and New 1950–1984*. New York: W.W. Norton & Company, 1984, p. 116.

——. 'Phantasia for Elvira Shatayev.' In *The Fact of a Doorframe: Poems Selected and New 1950–1984*. New York: W.W. Norton & Company, 1984, pp. 226–227.

——. *What Is Found There, Notebooks on Poetry and Poetics*. New York: W W Norton & Co., 1993.

Ricoeur, Paul. *Freedom & Nature: The Voluntary and the Involuntary*. Northwestern, 1966.

——. *Freud and Philosophy: An Essay on Interpretation*. New Haven, CT: Yale University Press, 1970.

——.'Creativity in Language'. Translated by David Pellauer. *Philosophy Today* 17 (Summer 1973).

——. *La Metaphor Vive*. Paris: Editions du Seuil, 1975.

——. 'Philosophical Hermeneutics and Theological Hermeneutics'. *Studies in Religion* No. 5 (1975–1976).

——. 'Imagination in Discourse and Action'. In *Analecta Husserliana: Yearbook of Phenomenological Research* Vol. 7 (1978).

——. 'The Metaphorical Process'. In *On Metaphor*. Edited by Sheldon Sacks. Chicago: The University of Chicago Press, 1978.

——. *The Ride of Metaphor: Multi-disciplinary Studies of the Creation of Meaning in Language*. London: Routledge & Kegan Paul, 1978

——. 'The Metaphorical Process as Cognition, Imagination and Feeling'. *Critical Inquiry* (1978–1979).

——. 'Towards a Hermeneutic of the Idea of Revelation'. In *Essays on Biblical Interpretation*. Edited by Lewis S. Nudge. Philadelphia: Fortress Press, 1980.

——. *Hermeneutics and the Human Sciences. Essays on Language, Actions and Interpretation*. Translated and edited by J. B. Thompson. Cambridge: Cambridge University Press, 1981.

——. 'On Interpretation'. In *Philosophy in France Today*. Edited by Alan Montefiore. Cambridge: Cambridge University Press, 1983.

——. *The Philosophy of Paul Ricoeur: An Anthology of His Work*. Edited by Rinpoche, Sogyal. *Meditation*. London: Rider, Ebuyr Press, 1994.

Ruddick, Sara. 'Remarks on Sexual Politics of Reason'. In *Women & Moral Theory*. Edited by E. Kittay & D. Meyers Towota. NJ: Rowman & Littlefield, 1987.

Ruether, Rosemary Radford. *Sexism and God-Talk. Toward a Feminist Theology*. Boston: Beacon Press, 1983.

Ruether, Rosemary. 'Imago Dei, Christian Tradition and Feminist Hermeneutics'. In *Image of God and Gender Models*. Edited by Kari Borresen. Oslo: Solum Forlag, 1991.

Rukeyser, Muriel. 'Letter to the Front'. In *The Collected Poems of Muriel Rukeyser*. Pittsburgh: University of Pittsburgh Press, 2005.

Sarton, May. 'Now I Become Myself' from *Collected Poems 1930–1993*. New York: W.W. Norton & Co., 1981.

Schrag, Calvin O. *Communicative Praxis and the Space of Subjectivity*. Bloomington: Indiana University Press, 1986.

Schutte, Ofelia. 'Irigaray on the Problem of Subjectivity'. *Hypatia* Vol. 6, No. 2.

Seller, Anne.'Whose Knowledge? Whose Post-Modernism?'. In *Women's Philosophy Review* No. 11 (1994).

Setter, Anne. 'Realism versus Relativism: Towards a Politically Adequate Epistemology'. In *Feminist Perspectives in Philosophy*. Edited by Morwenna Griffiths and Margaret Whitford. Indianapolis: Indiana University Press, 1988.

Shange, Ntozake. *For Colored Girls Who Have Considered Suicide When the Rainbow Is Enuf*. New York: Bantam Books, 1981.

Sloan, Douglas. *Insight-Imagination the Emancipation of Thought and the Modern World*. Connecticut: Greenwood Press, 1983.

Soskice, Janet Martin. 'Can a Feminist Call God "Father"?'. In *Speaking the Christian God: The Holy Trinity and the Challenge of Feminism*. Edited by Alvin F. Kimel, Jr. Michigan: Eerdman's Publishing Company, 1992.

Spender, Dale. *Man Made Language*. London: Routledge & Kegan Paul, 1980.

Spretnak, Charlene. *States of Grace: The Recovery of Meaning in the Postmodern Age*. New York: Harper Collins, 1993.

Stein, Edith. *The Problems of Women's Education, Edith Stein's Werke*, Vol. 5. Louvain Nauwelaerts & Freiburg: Herder, 1959.

Stevens, Wallace. *The Necessary Angel: Essays on Reality and the Imagination.*

Taylor, Owen. *What Coleridge Thought*. Middletown, CT: Wesleyan University Press, 1971.

Tertullian. *De Cultu Feminarium*. The Mud Flower Collective. *God's Fierce Whimsy: Christian Feminism and Theological Education*. New York: The Pilgrim Press, 1985.

Thistlethwaite, Susan. *Sex, Race & God: Christian Feminism in Black and White*. New York: Crossroad, 1989.

Tracy, David. *The Analogical Imagination: Christian Theology and the* Ungunmerr-Baumann, Miriam Rose and Brennan, Frank. 'Reverencing the Earth in the Australian Dreaming'. *The Way* (January, 1989).

Walker, Alice. *In Search of Our Mother's Gardens*. London: Women's Press, 1984.

Wamock, Mary. *Imagination*. London: Faber & Faber, 1976.

Watson, Gerard. *Phantasia in Classical Thought*. Galway: Galway University Press, 1988.

Weedon, Chris. *Feminist Practice and Poststructuralist Theory*. London: Basil Blackwell, 1987.

Welch, Sharon D. *A Feminist Ethic of Risk*. Minneapolis: Fortress Press, 1990.

White, Alan R. *The Language of Imagination*. Oxford: Basil Blackwell, 1990.

Whitford, Margaret. 'Irigaray's Body Symbolic'. Hypatia Vol. 6, No. 3 (Fall 1991): *Luce Irigaray: Philosophy in the Feminine*. London: Routledge, 1991.

Williams, Caroline. 'Feminism, Subjectivity and Psychoanalysis'. In *Knowing the Difference*. Edited by Kathleen Lennon and Margaret Whitford. London: Routledge, 1994.

Young, Iris Marion. *Justice and the Politics of Difference*. New Jersey: Princeton University Press, 1990.

Zappone, Katherine. '"Woman's Special Nature": A Different Horizon for Theological Anthropology'. Concilium, 1991.

——. *The Hope for Wholeness: A Spirituality for Feminists*. Mystic, CT: Twenty-Third Publications, 1991.

Index

www.ingramcontent.com/pod-product-compliance
Lightning Source LLC
Chambersburg PA
CBHW070426270326
41926CB00014B/2955
* 9 7 8 1 8 0 0 7 9 2 3 7 1 *